The Italian Wine Connoisseur

A 7-Day Guide to Mastering Italian Wines

E.V. Luther

I ❤ Italy.wine

THE ITALIAN WINE CONNOISSEUR

A SIMPLE 7-DAY GUIDE TO MASTERING ITALIAN WINES AND GRAPES; WITH THE CONFIDENCE AND EXPERTISE TO DRINK BOLDLY!

E.V. LUTHER

I ♥ Italy.wine

CONTENTS

ABOUT ILOVEITALY.WINE

The Iloveitaly.wine group is a small and perfectly formed bunch of friends, powered by wine and the flowing conversations and excellent life decisions it brings with it. We tour the supermarket aisles as well as wine regions of Italy and undertake wine courses and classes, to bring our digestible wine knowledge to readers who are also looking to make smarter decisions.. on wine of course, we can't help with it all.

Notwithstanding the gloriousness of many other alcoholic beverages, wine in all its majesty has no competition, and the desire to learn more and choose wisely, has united us as a group of friends and experts. We hope this book takes care of the geography of wine; gets you through a dinner choosing a decent one with a date; and also does a pretty good job on some of the grape and culture stuff as well. Enjoy, and cheers!

A FREE GIFT TO OUR READERS!

A 50 page Wine Tasting Journal with free guides on how to open a bottle; how to use an aroma wheel and more!

To get your free copy visit this link:
www.iloveitaly.wine/freejournal

INTRODUCTION

This seven-day guide aims to bring you a palatable, simple understanding of Italian wines, taking you from staring at a selection of distinctly average supermarket wines to being able to select, taste, pair and pour an outstanding Italian variety - all within a week. It will help you navigate the world of Italian wine, even if you are starting from zero knowledge - and a plane ticket to Italy is not required, but of course always encouraged. We all know how quickly a working week passes - imagine if by the time you close the laptop next Friday evening that your weekend tipple is an educated and informed decision of an excellent, sustainable wine, sourced through refined knowledge and taste. I certainly don't often make that kind of life progress in a week, so I'm happy to share my knowledge with you all so that you can.

A bottle of wine just **delivers**, on every level and for all social occasions; from dinner parties and 'let's sit down and chat' with your friends, to a present for the in-laws at Sunday lunch. Now we can't do anything about the fact that the latter might be a living hell with or without the wine, but we can at least make sure you earn some respect for the bottle clutched under your arm. Drinking and sharing wine is a central part of adult socialising and our generational culture that is just that little bit **even** more pleasurable if you know what on earth you're doing. And we plan to get you to exactly that point even if currently you don't know your Chianti from your Cortese.

So, first and foremost you will learn how to choose the right wine in the first place; from knowing Italian labels and regions, to knowing how to taste wine with confidence, choose the right bottle for the right occasion and then; pair it with the right types of foods. Again, if your capabilities in the kitchen department are terrible in the first place, then we can't work miracles here guys, and I suggest a simple cookbook would be a good idea to compliment this guide. I certainly rely on one. The ability to choose the right wines to match food courses is undeniably the pinnacle of adulting, it gets no higher than that - should you wish to take this further to what is, let's face it, a genius level of wine expertise, we share more resources at the end of the book and through our website www.iloveitaly.wine.

And at that point you may as well quit your dayjob and make it your living - I know I would. For now, we aim to bring you our most easy-to-use and digestible wine knowledge to help you make smarter decisions and be just that little bit more equipped - all in time for the weekend.

The benefits of adopting the techniques and knowledge shared in this book are that you will be able to choose wines more cleverly, and much as the title suggests, have the confidence to drink boldly.

An added bonus is the comprehensive understanding of the geography of wine, and a wider appreciation of the grapes and ageing process - and if you're anything like me then an advancement in any geography knowledge is never a bad thing.

It will probably also help guide your next Italian holiday destination let's face it - think dreamy wineries and rolling hills instead of pokey AirBnBs and packed bars you've read about in a Lonely Planet from ten years ago.

Once you know the labels and terroirs of Italy to look for, you'll never look back. We hope the knowledge gained in this book also gets you through a dinner party or a date being able to choose a decent bottle of wine with ease - we can't be a dating agency either, I'm afraid, but we do know this is one of the scariest scenarios to declare your wine ignorance and we feel your pain.

And don't even get me started on how satisfying it is to sit in a high-end restaurant with work colleagues able to choose from the ever-intimidating wine list and know what you are talking about. Satisfaction never tasted so sweet. Or was it dry?

To look specifically at Italian wine, you will need a basic understanding of their wine labelling world - Italy has more grape varieties than any other country and its naming practice is done through the DOC (Demoni-nazione di Origine Controllata) classification system, with an added layer standing for 'guaranteed' or 'garan-tita' in Italian - i.e "DOGC" Denominazione di Origine Controllata e Garantita."

When a wine has this as its classification, it is consid-ered the highest accolade that Italian wines can be awarded. The classification means that there are controlled production methods (controllata) and then guaranteed wine quality (garantita) with each bottle, which is seen to verify its namesake - "controlled and guaranteed designation of origin." *(The 24-hour wine expert, 2017)* Basically you're drinking the good stuff.

Before we get stuck in, just to explain the process - at the end of each chapter I plan to cover one label of specially-sourced Italian wine each day, for all of the seven days to follow - so if you plan to follow this guide to the letter, then you are welcome to order the 7 bottles of wine in the table below beforehand, to taste daily as we proceed with our step-by-step guide.

This will be a huge benefit to not only having a particularly pleasurable week, but also in understanding the flavours and wine-tasting techniques to which I refer in the following chapters.

Where possible I will refer to other equivalent varieties or certainly let you know the wine type so you can get your hands on similar.

List of Wines for the week

Day 1: Red	Day 2: White	Day 3: Red	Day 4: Red	Day 5: White	Day 6: White	Day 7: Red
La Ghirlanda Chianti Classico, 2018.	Elibaria Vermentino di Gallura DOCG, 2021.	Rosso di Montalcino DOC, 2019.	Masciarelli Marina Cvetic Riserva, 2016.	Laguna, 100% Turbiana -Pratello Lombardy, 2019.	Feudi di San Gregorio Falanghina, 2021.	Teroldego Rotaliano Riserva, Castel Firmian, 2018.

DAY 1

AN INTRODUCTION TO ITALY AND ITALIAN WINE PRODUCTION

Italy is practically synonymous with wine, even more so than it is with pasta, beautiful women and those tiny Fiat 500s or Vespas that you can't help but be amazed anybody is still driving. And it is not only seemingly the destination of choice for a generation of us obsessed with getting an Insta shot on Positano's colourful rolling tiered hills, or seeing if the adorable fishing village of Portofino descended on by the masses can possibly be **that** beautiful; it is also, quite rightfully, now seen as a wine-producing powerhouse. Italy's standing as such, continues to grow year on year, and for those of us wanting to make wine choices based on actual confidence of the quality, this is more than just 'fantastico' news.

More than 400 types of grapes are now grown across 20 winemaking regions in Italy *(Wine Market News, 2019)* helping Italy to take the global top spot in terms of the amount of wine produced - it currently accounts for roughly one-fifth of the world's wine. *(Wine Enthusiast, 2010)* Let's take a moment to appreciate that, considering the size of this tiny boot-shaped pocket rocket - and puts it second only to Spain when it comes to wine exports. That is no small feat considering a country like Argentina which also goes pretty hard on the wine production front, is 823% larger than Italy. We will cover the wine regions of Italy in detail on Day 3, but for now it is important to know that the 20 distinct regions spread across 695,000 hectares. *(Vineyards.com 2020)*

Now that Italy is reaching its potential for the quality and amount of wine produced each year, it was recently crowned the *best destination in the world for wine lovers.* Need I say more - there is quite literally a title bestowed upon a country for its excellence in this arena, and people like you and I intend to celebrate it. What's more, in 2019 the regions of Congegliano and Valdobbiadene – home to the country's renowned Prosecco – were added to the UNESCO World Heritage List. *(Wine Market News, 2019)* I will pop my cork to that any day.

Now let's take a look at the multi-millennia-old history of wine that has shaped Italy into the dynamo wine producer it is today. Wine has been part of Italian culture since the peninsula was colonised by the Ancient Greeks. It is as much part of their culture as Parmigiano-Reggiano is to pasta - but even thousands of years before that (now, my history gets sticky here) if research is to be believed. So when the Greeks first arrived in their boot-shaped heaven in the 8th century BC, they brought with them, I assume in addition to a pretty feral boat, the true art of winemaking as we know it today. In fact the Mycenaean Greeks have been attributed to this technique in all its glory, introducing viticulture first to Sicily and then to Southern Italy *(Masterclass, 2020)* They honed their winemaking prowess as a matter of urgency, and nicknamed the land that had so impressed them, as "Oenotria," or 'the land of trained vines' in English *(Via Verde, 2017)*

Later, while these Etruscans were busy winemaking in central Italy, the Romans defeated the Carthaginians (again, where was I in that history lesson?) and built slave-run plantations in coastal areas as well, spreading the wine trade country-wide. As such, wine became as much a central part of everyday life, as I can only assume chariot-racing and gladiator shows. Combine those three and I think you'd still have a pretty epic weekend. In fact, the wild festivals that celebrated the

Roman god Bacchus, got so out of hand that they were eventually banned by the Roman Senate and huge wine consumption can't have helped tame things - not so dissimilar to the modern-day after all. Jump forward through the Middle Ages to AD 92, and Emperor Domitian was forced to destroy a large number of vineyards in order to free up land for (arguably more important) food and farming production. *(Masterclass, 2020)*

Much like everything 'Roman,' their wine was much stronger than the equivalent we know today. Due to its high alcohol content it was therefore usually diluted with water, which seems a cardinal sin by a culture we now see as an authority on dining etiquette but there you go, history teaches us some tough lessons indeed. The Romans also preferred sweet wines and favoured white over red, and would often add unusual flavours such as honey, salt and herbs in a bid to modify its taste. *(Masterclass, 2020)* Essentially you get my gist - there is hope for refinement and knowledge to your wine etiquette no matter what your starting point.

Credit where credit is due, the Romas are to thank for many contributions to contemporary winemaking and production techniques that may otherwise have gone undiscovered, like presses for extracting juice, and storing it in wooden barrels to perfect the acquired aged taste. They also forged the foundations of what is widely considered standard winemaking wisdom (soon to be your own), using methods to taste and grow grapes properly and learn more about climate and terroir. Cleverly, or slyly depending on how you see it, wine viticulture outside of Italy was prohibited under Roman law throughout this time, and they had a monopoly on its production. All exports to other areas and countries were made in exchange for slaves. (*Wine Market News, 2019*) Once these laws were relaxed, vineyards began to flourish throughout the rest of Europe, now finally able to grow their grapes freely and join the party.

Then, in the nineteenth century, the vine louse 'phylloxera' took hold and destroyed many of Italy's vineyards along with much of Northern Europe's. I won't go into too much further detail on this as louse varieties are sadly another weak subject area of mine, but know that it wasn't good and it killed everything in its path. Picture your slugs in the garden during summer and not being able to get rid of the little pests. After 'louse-gate,' the replanted vineyards were often designed with quantity, not quality in mind, and we all know the results of that unfavourable approach. Italy became a global source of inexpensive table wines. We all know them; we've all drunk them; and we've all had the headache the next morning but a fun memory to show for it. These have their place in our lives, but let's all be pleased that quality was regained in the 1960's (now we're talking, some of us are on our way into the world about now) when a series of laws were passed to control wine quality, labelling and production - and it is then that the modern era of respected Italian wine-making began. We will look into exactly what this classification system does tomorrow, but for now you know it is the divide of before and after for Italian wine.

Take, for example, the elegance of Gaja Barbaresco wine, which uses the grape variety 'Nebbiolo,' (we'll get to that properly later as well) and is still managed as a family business. This is a distinct and respected wine for the unique characteristics of its Italian terroir and customers' trust in the brand. Angelo Gaja is at the helm of communicating the family story and he has paved the way since his ancestors of the 1800's to produce quality, opulent wines. But when he came aboard in 1961, during this new era of Italian wine-making, he immediately set out to reduce yields in the vineyards and introduce small oak barrels. His other missions were to use more expert knowledge to identify different vineyard sites and vinify them separately in the first place. *(Wine Enthusiast 2010)* What he did was pave the way for a respected reputation for quality and production at his own estate, as well as help other

Italian families in the same roles to change how they do things. The result in the case of this label, is a seriously impressive flavour with notes of berry fruits and soft spice that is a great example of quality improvement.

Another wine that comes to mind when thinking about the 'new age' after the 1960's is Tenuta San Guido Sassicaia. 'Sassicaia' is a name to become familiar with from this book, as it put Italy on the world enological* map (*think wine map but a fancier word) soon after it was first introduced in 1968.

Practically a straightforward Cabernet Sauvignon but with a small percent of Cabernet Franc, from coastal Tuscany, this wine put Italy on a par with the Premier Cru wines of Bordeaux and Italy on the wine map forevermore. Tenuta San Guido is today managed by Nicolò Rocchetta *(Wine Enthusiast 2010)* and their wine is considered the 'seminal super Tuscan' - a term we will use from here as well. Now, not to get caught up with credited wine experts and start a great wine debate, but many wine critics would vote this as Italy's number one red. I will leave you to sample this and decide for yourself, but I do know it will show you complex herbal notes of chopped mint, licorice and bramble - and if you can detect all of those after seven days together, you will be doing pretty well. From the get-go, it is undoubtedly essential to the story of Italy's wine reputation movement.

And finally for today as an example to wet your appetite; one of the oldest and most established wineries in Vulture, D'Angelo, which is to this day, a family-run business. Its beginnings were focused around quantity - an original story told above and echoed across southern Italy - until the 1950s, when it began to bottle only its quality, rich and concentrated wine under the Casa Vinicola D'Angelo label. (Wine Enthusiast, 2021)

Vinification of their red wines follows the same traditional methods in the winery's large concrete tanks that were constructed all those years ago, but with a focus on bottling better quality. It was one of the first wineries to produce bottles labelled as Aglianico del Vulture DOC and shifted to one of the most sophisticated Italian wine brands by the family's fourth generation at the helm today. These are a sister-brother duo: Erminia, who runs the commercial side of the business, and Rocco, the winemaker and vineyard manager. (Wine Enthusiast, 2021) Considering my brother and I can't organise a family lunch without an argument, I'd say this is a pretty impressive sibling feat and represents the true nature of family-orientated Italian culture still flourishing to this day.

Now that we know a few of the family stories and I have shamelessly name-dropped some labels, you will be starting to understand how the Italian wines we see today are more varied, more refined, and more popular than ever, and have come a long way since 50 years ago. Deservingly, thanks to the focus on ethical quality and dedication to new production methods that have taken place over that time, reputation has shifted on its axel and Italy now leads the way in best practise. Hundreds of *varietals (*get used to a new word basically meaning 'varieties' which I also use) planted every year and many of these are grown only in Italy, which gives us an exciting opportunity to celebrate the gloriously sophisticated and specific realm of modern-day Italian wine. As if anyone said 'research' had to be boring..

For your pleasure, and most definitely ours, we have therefore selected 7 Italian wines to take you on this journey through a week-long tasting guide to take place at the end of each day, as they have been specifically selected from a narrative of the history and evolution of Italian wine. These are the defining wines of Italy you are likely to already know a little about - but after seven days on the good stuff you will be able to identify the quality and craftsmanship from individual distinct terroirs. We will work logically through a seven-day period, and end with that most magnificent of a red Sunday tipple by the fire (ignore if it's summer where you are). This journey together represents at least a small piece of the wider definition of 'Vino Italiano' which is ultimately how Italians live the 'Dulce Vita' we are all after - I'd have a sweet life too if I drank excellent wine all day in the sunshine. This journey will show you some of the delicious reds, easy whites and punchy sparkling wines made in every style from traditional to ultra-modern, and teach you the essentials along the way.

DAY 1 WINE

So, we are staring down the barrel (see what I did there) of Day 1 and a blissful week ahead of trying a different, new and exciting wine every evening - not to alienate those of you drinking at lunchtime however, that deserves the utmost respect. Let's start with our Day 1 wine; A typically elegant, sophisticated and built to age bottle as any we would expect from the Italians - giving you an immediate sense of the classic iconic variety of wines we celebrate them for - the *'La Ghirlanda Chianti Classico 2018.'* "La Ghirlanda" means "The Crown" in English, for those of us not counting fluency in Italian among our skillset, so basically this translates as the King of Chianti Classico.

The best of the best. The 'classico' in this context just means it is a classic growing zone within a particular region - more on the regions on Day 3 but for now don't worry about it and get stuck in. It doesn't mean the wine is **necessarily** any better, just that it's from a 'classic' wine growing area and they are not doing anything extraordinary to change or diversify the grape. *(Wine Enthusiast, 2010)* If you're trying this exact brand, you will find it a medium ruby shade in colour, and you should be detecting classic dark fruits, rosemary and balsamic notes.

The producers are the Bindi Sergardi family, who have been producing wine for 23 generations from the district of Monteriggioni ever since the estate was built at the end of the 15th century, so it is no wonder this is the outstanding result. The vineyard covers a hundred hectares of utter wine heaven, and is structured around three of the prestigious DOCGs mentioned above in our introduction; Chianti, Chianti Colli Senesi and Chianti Classico. *(Vinatis 2020)* This winehouse continues to produce outstanding wines, with expertise passed down for hundreds of years; "a true and authentic expression of Sangiovese" - i.e. the leading grape for this territory. (More on this grape type too later, but it's a big one)

It is a well-balanced first wine to get your head around and a medium-body, so nothing too rich as we take off on this journey together.. let's save that for Day 7 and your well-oiled expertise. It is easy to drink and very enjoyable, so don't be surprised if you have more than a glass for the sake of research. It is about £20 (US$25) and very accessible to buy, but a few more Chianti Classico suggestions that will deliver outstanding quality as well, based on similar taste, price and community ratings online, include the following:

- Antinori Péppoli Chianti Classico 2018; approximately £12 (US$15)
- Poggio Bonelli Chianti Classico Reserva 2017; approximately £23 (US$28)
- Chianti Classico Riserva - I Colli 2016 - Bindi Sergardi; approximately £27 (US$33) from the same wine family
- Barone Ricasoli Castello di Brolio Chianti Classico - Castello di Brolio represents 16 years of research and investment to produce a "grand cru" wine that is a true expression of Brolio terroir *(Wine Enthusiast, 2010)*

The wine 'type' itself, Chianti Classico, is well-known for delivering elegance and intensity, with aromas that are immediately released by pouring it into the glass; helping us learners feel we can detect the fruity and balsamic notes straight away, even with our novice noses. Let's celebrate those great iconic families of the wine world here again; This time the Ricasoli family; who are credited with inventing the original formula for Chianti Classico (Sangiovese with Canaiolo and Malvasia grapes) that is used today with a minimum 80% Sangiovese *(Wine Enthusiast, 2010)* Without the late Barone Bettino Ricasoli who only died in 2009, and his relatives before him, the world would be without this utmost food-friendly wine. Chianti Classico is an Italian landmark wine and Castello di Brolio's success has spanned the 20th century and beyond. *(Wine Enthusiast, 2010)* It set the baseline standard for other Chianti Classicos to follow, from Castello di Fonterutoli, Rocca delle Macie, Felsina, San Felice, Badia a Coltibuono, Carpineto and Castello di Albola among others - all certainly worth a drink in their own right and ones for your lists.

Chianti Classico received DOC status in 1967 and then DOCG in 1984 *(Consorzio Vino, 2020)* officially ranking it a product of excellence in the national and international wine sector. Classically it will exhibit rich notes of berry fruit, spice and blackberry, and is incredibly smooth and polished in the mouth, with silky tannins and an enduring finish. It is a wine that lines the palate, embellishes aromas and certainly glorifies and celebrates its foods.

Now, what foods to pair it with? We will get to wine pairing later on as we learn more each day, but for Day 1 let's keep this simple and mention that the everyday dinner foods that go well with this wine are beef, and veal in particular, or even poultry. That keeps it fairly straightforward to match a Day 1 meal to your first bottle of expertly chosen wine - so bon appétit my wine-smart friends.

DAY 1 TAKEAWAY LESSON; HOW TO OPEN A BOTTLE OF WINE PROPERLY AND WHY

We have all been there; a gorgeous dinner party with friends and somebody asks you to crack open the first bottle of wine for the evening. Assuming these are close enough friends to admit your ignorance and defeat, you would do much like I did for years and meekly admit you are terrible at it and pass it onto the nearest willing friend, only too happy to appear far more worldly... eurgh. Well, I am pleased to tell you that really, it isn't difficult, and for those of us navigating far more challenging jobs, social lives and even children - I can assure you, you've got this. First of all it helps to get your hands on a "waiter's friend" style corkscrew like the below:

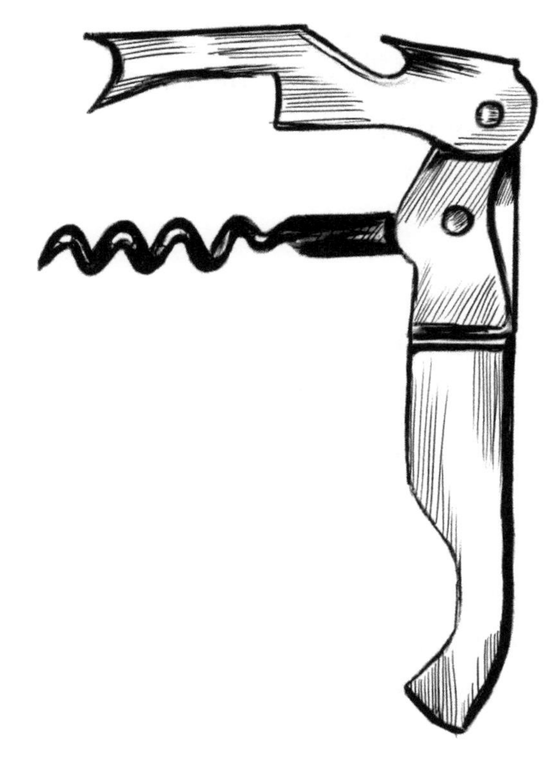

Fig 1. A waiter's friends corkscrew

They are widely available at most supermarkets or wine / kitchen shops and cost about £10. Don't be tempted to hang on to that friends' freebie silver corkscrew that was a favour at a wedding seven years ago, as it's just not going to cut the mustard now you're an expert. That said, you don't need to go too fancy either - this variety of corkscrew, as favoured by restaurants as the standard tool, will outperform other alternatives even in its most basic form and already makes you look like you know what you're doing. Make sure it has a serrated blade, (much like your finest bread knife) as it's important in cutting the foil smoothly and will be useless without it. We need to start as we mean to go on here.

Once you have the precious cargo in arms, or more accurately, safely on a kitchen worktop - follow the below 5 basic steps to opening the bottle correctly:

The Right Way to Open a Bottle of Wine (Wine Folly, 2020)

1. Hold the bottle still and on a flat surface
2. Cut the foil below the lower lip across the front, back, and top of the foil (At the risk of sounding like your mother here, keep your fingers clear of the blade and the foil)
3. Set the screw to just off-centre of the cork and insert, rotating straight into it (now isn't the time to let fear take over, just got for it)
4. Rotate the corkscrew 6 half turns clockwise, and you should be left looking at only one turn of the corkscrew still showing
5. Lever the cork out slowly on the first step, then the second, and then finally ease the cork out with your hand - this is when you get the

delicious 'pop' sound and you know you've made it

6. Wipe off any sediment with a napkin ensuring any mess later on has absolutely nothing to do with you

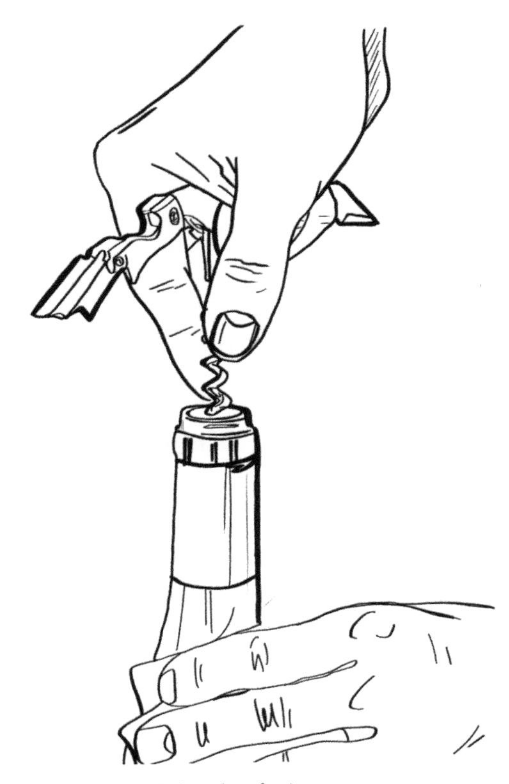

Fig 2. How to open a cork bottle of wine

SUMMARY OF DAY 1

Now I hope that as we come to the end of Day 1 you are excited to start exploring Italian wines for the week ahead, and find the best bottles for your (up until this point maybe rather average) collection? As well as an introduction to the types of wines you find across the 20 winemaking regions of the country, we also learned today about Italy's incredible capacity in sheer exports and an introduction to a few of the names that emerge in specific regions.

We have also covered a general understanding of the 4000 year-old history of wine production in Italy and how it leads us to the present-day, as well as how wine has been a part of Italian culture even long before the Romans further promoted it. Then, in the 1960s, we learned that the laws passed for quality of wines gave way to the modern era of Italian winemaking that we know today.

I have introduced you briefly to the grape varieties that are grown here, as well as a few classic flagship wines that Italian winemaking owes its reputation to.

As we popped our first cork on Day 1 together, we tried the incredible 'La Ghirlanda Chianti Classico 2018' as our opening must-try, and learned about its famous wine type 'Chianti Classico' known for its elegance and intensity. Add to that your new-found ability to open a bottle properly and you're almost flying.

So as we approach the end of the first day (exhausted anyone?) this opening day has been an introduction to set the scene of Italian winemaking and explain what is to follow in the following six chapters. Think of this book as a sort of pocket-guide to becoming a connoisseur of Italian wine; soon to be armed with the knowledge of Italy's wine regions, what grapes to look for, what wines are produced in the distinctive different areas, and what bottles get our vote while you enjoy trying them all to see if you agree.

Onwards to Day 2 my wine-loving friends…

DAY 1 GLOSSARY OF TERMS

Enology - wine making

Terroir - region

Vintner - winemaker / producer

The Appellation System in Italy:

Vini DOP stands for "Denominazioni di Origine Protetta": Wines with Protected Designation of Origin with premium DOCG wines

Vini Varietali means Varietal Wines with at least 85% of the wine made from one of a list of international grape varieties: Merlot, Chardonnay, Cabernet Sauvignon, Syrah, Sauvignon Blanc and Cabernet Franc etc

Vini for generic wines

DAY 2

THE ITALIAN WINE PYRAMID AND APPELLATION SYSTEM

HISTORY

When Italy became one nation in 1861, the rules relating to the wine world were certainly not equally uniformed, and arguably weren't the highest thing on the agenda at that point. Upon the Unification of Italy, wine became "Italian wine" and was owned by a united country finally, although the concept of a region let alone territory of origin, was still lacking. *(My Name is Barbera, 2017)* Looking now at the history of Italian Wines with Designation of Origin in our understanding, it appears governments of the newly-formed Italian nation (starting as early as 1885) were concerned solely with the authenticity of wines, and the classifications that reflect it.

The first sign of change took place in 1930, when a regulation was issued for the protection of Italian wine productions. *(My Name is Barbera, 2017)* The Ministry of Agriculture was tasked with recognising and defining the areas of production of these wines, as well as a basic level of classification of these products in three distinct levels for the so-called below "Typical" (i.e. traditional local) wines, namely:

- Special Wines; (i.e. good)
- Superior Wines; (i.e. really good)
- Fine Wines. (i.e. exceptional)

In 1963 a landmark wine moment took place, a 'wine-ment' if you will, with the enactment of Presidential Decree No. 930 on the Protection of Wine Designations of Origin, i.e DOC, the first national measure governing quality wine productions, defining its origin and strengthening the concept of tie with the territory. *(My Name is Barbera, 2017)* This law set strict rules in place regarding the production and marketing of wines; including specifications on designation; the creation of specially provided registers for the recording of production surfaces and; a system of reporting the quantity of grapes produced to be destined for the production of a particular designation. The law also laid down a new system of classification of wines to advance the above - it would from then be distinguished as:

- Wine with simple Designation of Origin;
- Wine with Controlled Designation of Origin;
- Wine with Controlled Designation of Origin Guaranteed.

The first of these classifications was granted to the Vernaccia di San Gimignano label, soon followed by other designation labels including Brunello di Montalcino, which in 1980 then was also the first to receive recognition as a DOCG wine *(My Name is Barbera, 2017).*

The introduction of this regulation had huge impacts on the qualitative and quantitative aspect of Italian wine, and is the real point in history we begin to celebrate it as we know it today.

In the early 1990's the wine growing and production industry had to take action to ensure a limit to the considerable growth in the number of DOC wines and the new market requirements. i.e. there was too much of a good thing.

It wasn't long before in 1993 a new law was issued with new and stricter innovations in the field. The new innovations to the law included *(My Name is Barbera 2017)*

- Activity of enhancement of designations;
- Introduction of IGT wines which we will cover below ('Indicazioni Geografiche Tipiche' i.e. 'typical wines')
- Geographical Indication;
- Harvest selection allowing production of the same vineyard for several DOCs;
- Recognition of sub-regions, i.e. more restricted areas within the DOC; and
- Mandatory introduction of chemical-physical analyses before marketing.

But the real impact of this law of the early 1990's lies in its bearing quality in terms of origin and which was given shape through the mechanism of the pyramidal classification of wines as we know it today.

Based on this historical background, the modern-day European Community of 2008 implemented a process of reform for the entire wine growing and production industry. *(My Name is Barbera, 2017)*

Known as, and with absolutely no charm, as Regulation No. 479, the reform was introduced to bring new rules of governance to production and marketing, labelling, defence and promotion of designations. This was both on the international market as well as a tracking system that each Member State in Italy must adhere to, and may apply for independently as a further guarantee for consumers. *(My Name is Barbera, 2017)*

The reform plan of 2009 also aimed at simplifying the legal framework, adopting more transparent rules and equating the wine growing and production legislation with those already in place for other quality agricultural and food product supply chains with a DOP and IGP labelling in place. *(My Name is Barbera, 2017)*

The result is only two distinguished categories of wine, known from 2009 onwards as:

- Wines with Geographical Indication (DOP and IGP)
- Wines without Geographical Indication (generic wines or with just the indication of the vine)

The Italian State has allowed the continued use of 'old' acronyms which characterised the Italian quality wines previously (DOCG [CGDO], DOC. [CDO] and IGT [TGI]), which can be either written together with the new ones or alone - it is these classic acronyms I will use for the sake of consistency in this book and to avoid even more confusion than changing the laws and labels hundreds of times for you.

PRE 2009

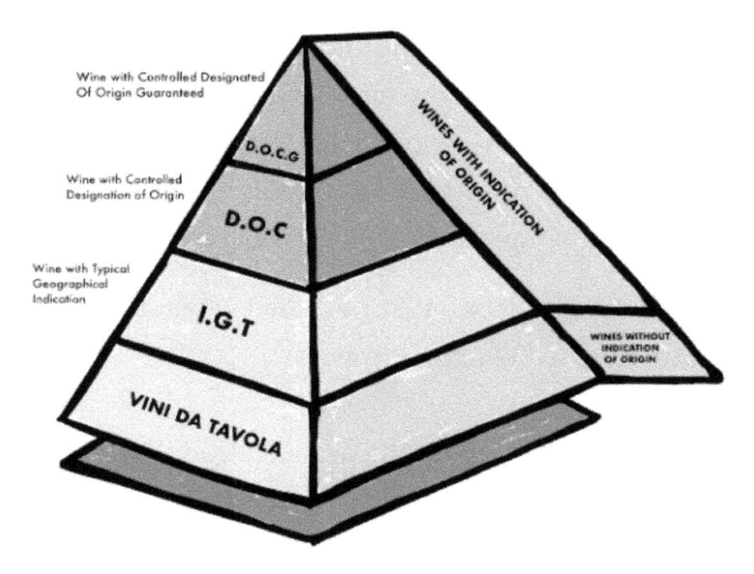

Fig 3. Italian Wine Pyramid and Appelation system

The Italian Wine Pyramid is the way in which wine is characterised by the laws in place to indicate its quality. (*My name is Babera, 2017*) Essentially, there are four classifications that make up the above "Pyramid of Quality." The highest quality wines (let's be clear here in this circumstance means characterised by strict production rules and the highest value) are at the top of the pyramid, working down towards the base where the lowest "quality wines" are characterised by meeting the fewest restrictions and lowest value.

DOCG

The Denominazione di Origine Controllata e Garantita (DOCG) as covered briefly in the Introduction, is Italy's highest wine classification. These wines have the deepest relationship with their production areas and will be traceable to a specific region, according to strict rules, and are likely to have those family-owned traditions and heritage stories we have read a little about before now. Some outstanding examples of what are already the most highly classified wine labels are Barbera d'Asti, Barolo and Brunello di Montalcino.

The DOCG wine rules are more stringent than those for one level below in our wine pyramid, namely the DOC wines. The yield of grapes is lower; additional labelling is required, and the wine must be aged longer for the top dogs. To obtain the 'G' of the DOCG as outlined in the introduction meaning 'guaranteed,' the wine must have been certified DOC for at least ten years, and it really is a case of age being more than just a number. DOCG wines are also sealed with a numbered governmental stamp across the cork which is not obligatory for the DOC. This stamp on the bottle is the guarantee of productions with strict adherence to the Italian local wine rules. *(My name is Barbera, 2017)*

DOCG appellations are often identified with small areas such as valleys, hills, and municipalities. For example the below:

- Moscato di Scanzo DOCG, which is the smallest Italian denomination, refers to a part of the municipality of Scanzorosciate, in Lombardy; Franciacorta DOCG refers to the Franciacorta wine area, a specific hilly area;
- Brunello di Montalcino DOCG refers to the municipality of Montalcino, in Tuscany;
- Vermentino di Gallura DOCG refers to a geographical area in the north-east of Sardinia (there might just be more on this one in store for Day 2)

(Italiano wine, 2018)

It is not possible to acquire the DOCG appellation without first having a lower level classification from the below. In fact, the DOCG mark is reserved exclusively for:

- Recognised DOC wines and products in well-defined areas;
- Typologies of wine belonging to an appellation DOC for at least 10 years;
- Particularly valuable wines, both for the qualitative characteristics and the commercial reputation;
- Status made by at least fifty-one percent of the subjects leading vineyards and representing at least fifty-one percent of the total area

(Italiano wine, 2018)

Since these wines are the best of the best, let's spend a bit longer on what sets them apart and which wines can be included.. The DOCG appellation can (somewhat confusingly at this stage but bear with me) include two further classification levels that allow specific identification of territory. These are as follows:

- The sotto-zone (meaning sub-zones in Italian), intended as portions of territory;
- The vigneti (vineyards in Italian), intended as single plots of land;

- More restrictive quality constraints, which must be explicitly indicated in the reference specification, and;
- Both levels can be reported on the label with the relevant mentions.

(Italiano wine, 2018)

DOC

Denominazione di Origine Controllata, or DOC, is the next level down in the wine pyramid. A wine marked DOC is produced in a specific, well-defined region according to strict wine-making rules designed to preserve the local traditions and is still an extremely highly respected bracket of Italian wine. Both DOCG and DOC are the categories that fall under the EU's "Quality Wine Produced in a Specific Area" definition.

In this sense, a "specific area" means that produced in a "well-defined geographical area with precise chemical and organoleptic characteristics which have been established in advance according to the specific production criteria." *(My name is Barbera, 2017)* Nobody can accuse them of being vague here I guess.

A great nod to an ethical supply chain and a family paying homage to producing excellent DOC marked wine, is the Paternoster winery - under the helm of Fabio Mecca.

Founded by Anselmo Paternoster in 1925, this historic winery is one of the defining pillars of Vulture, and is now a leader in bringing a more modern wine production style to the area.

Anselmo's son, Pino, was one of the first formally trained vintners in the area of his time, and moved it towards modernity in the 1970s, when he led the charge along with other historic wineries, like D'Angelo, to bottle 'Aglianico' wine with the newly approved DOC labelling and standards.

Today, the winery is led by Fabio, fourth generation of the Paternoster family, who continues the legacy producing a range of Aglianico and Falanghina DOC from 50 acres of organic vineyards throughout Barile. *(Wine Enthusiast, 2022)*

It is worth being clear that the specifications around criteria to make a wine DOC marked, determine the actual types of wine that can be produced in the first place, Tipologia, Riserva, or Superiore; as well as the varieties of grapes that can be used and the permitted yield of these grapes per hectare.

It also determines the conversion efficiency of grapes into wine (usually at an alcohol percentage of 70%) and the type and duration of ageing.

Italian law also requires that the DOC wines' quality be controlled, so before being allowed on the market, the wines undergo chemical analyses to ensure they meet the Disciplinare di Produzione's standards. *(My name is Barbera, 2017)*

IGT

Indicazione Geografica Tipica (IGT) translates as "Typical Geographical Indication," and are the next step down from DOC wines, forming a large middle chunk of the classification.

IGT indicates the name of a region or a specific location and is used to describe a wine from that region that has determined qualities, reputation or other characteristics that are attributed specifically to it.

They are not as specific as the above DOC wines and the main, and almost only specific, features of the wine other than the geographical area from which it originated (for example Latium or Veneto), are; the base grape variety (for example Chardonnay) and the vintage year.

At least 85% of these wines are named after the geographical area they derived from.

Finally, IGT wines must meet certain parameters that are indicated by production regulations, such as: *(Feder Doc, 2022)*

- the maximum yield of grapes per hectare;
- the transformation yield of grapes into wine;
- the minimum natural alcoholic proof;
- the alcoholic strength for consumption;
- the vines from which they can be obtained.

For this group it is said that the demarcation of the wine-making grapes has been introduced, which means that it will no longer be possible to produce a wine with IGT from grapes that are harvested in one region but vinified in another; except for the 15% of the grapes that can come from outside the area. In addition to that, IGT wines are still subjected to stringent control procedures. *(Feder Doc, 2022)*

To add more confusion, this same large group of classified wines is sometimes referenced as IGP (or PGI in English) since 2009 as well, translating to "Protected Geographical Indication" rather than 'Typical' but refers to exactly the same classification and is interchangeable as a term.

VINI VARIETALI

At the base of the pyramid, and for the sake of distinguishing the classifications, we have the lowest quality standard - Vini Varietali. Varietali means a wine produced from a specific grape variety which is mostly printed on the label for all to see as it is.

Their label can show a reference to the vintage and / or the variety of grapes used but is fairly vague - and Vini Varietali itself on the label tells you only that the wine is made in Italy, and they are mostly made to be consumed in local regions.

The more detailed indication on the label of the vine is limited to only a few varieties in this category: namely Cabernet, Cabernet Franc, Cabernet Sauvignon, Chardonnay, Merlot, Sauvignon, Syrah.

These are also post-2009 sometimes simply called the 'generic wines,' due to having no origin indication and are wines that can be produced with grapes from different areas and / or from different Member States. *(My name is Barbera, 2017)*

Since 2009, the European Community has reformed the wine classification system to equate the wine growing and production legislation with the ones already existing for the rest of the agricultural and food products. Now only two classifications are provided:

- Wines with geographical indication, DOP and IGP
- Wines without geographical indication, Vini varietali

Note: Italy allows the continued use of the traditional designations to characterise quality wines. DOCG and DOC both correspond to DOP; IGT corresponds to IGP. *(My name is Barbera, 2017)*

THE WINE AROMA WHEEL

The Wine Aroma Wheel is the essential tool to use as you grow and enhance your wine knowledge, and is the way in which you will begin to understand aroma complexity in the aromas of your fine Italian wines.

It is the tool of choice for educators to help wine lovers discern the different aromatic nuances and wine *(The Wine Aroma Wheel.com, 2022)* and a useful tool for the evolving wine lover to have on hand while wine tasting which we will get to in later chapters - and acts as a visual glossary of wine terms, organised by origin.

Fig 4. Ann Noble's Aroma Wheel (1987)

Access to a digital colour version like the above (we create this version- maybe sell it on the website)

The purpose of the Wine Aroma Wheel is to help you easily identify different aromas in wine, with the help of a colour-coded visual aid. Wine aromas are moderately complex, and (more likely as your expertise grows) it is possible to detect up to several hundred aroma compounds within a single glass of wine.

To make things even more interesting (/challenging in the meantime) the different aroma compounds can interact with other aromas to create new and more complex aromas. With just a bit of practise and your own wine aroma wheel on hand, this becomes a well-nurtured skill in order to finely detect multiple aromas in all types of wine.

WINE AROMA WHEEL HISTORY

During America's wine boom in the 1970s, a wine professor at the University of California named Ann Noble, identified the need for a common tasting vocabulary to be used by the wine industry. (*"How Robert Parker's 90+ and Ann Noble's Aroma Wheel Changed the Discourse of Wine Tasting Notes," Open Edition, 2018*) In 1984 she created the original Wine Aroma Wheel containing over eighty aroma descriptors as above.

The Wine Wheel became a commercial success, as well as a useful tool for the everyday wine drinker as well as experts in the field.

Up until this point, wine terminology had been a more general glossary of terms - words which you and I would use today and not as accurate to distinguish between properties.

Before the Wine Wheel existed for this purpose, figures such as French wine merchant André Simon, oenologist Émile Peynaud, and British auctioneer Michael Broadbent had compiled their own glossaries of acceptable wine terminology, *("How Robert Parker's 90+ and Ann Noble's Aroma Wheel Changed the Discourse of Wine Tasting Notes," Open Edition, 2018)* that were all heavily influenced by their respective backgrounds and biassed to their professions.

Not everyone agreed with the move towards greater specialisation even by the time Ann Noble created her more detailed Wine Wheel, and even close colleagues of hers had been warning against it since the mid-1970s.

Words like "nutty", "chalky" and "nuance" had been reference in their list of taboos as wine language evolved, because they were deemed too precise, and not immediately comprehensible. (*"How Robert Parker's 90+ and Ann Noble's Aroma Wheel Changed the Discourse of Wine Tasting Notes," Open Edition, 2018*)

Eight years later these very terms were included in Noble's wheel and are still very much used to this day as common wine terms. They are indicative of the refined (yes this includes you now) preference for specialised, precise aroma descriptors over simple and overarching terminology.

How to use an aroma wheel

The quickest way to learn how to use your wheel is to first line up a selection of wines (shame) to practise identifying all the different flavours on the wheel.

Start with selecting two or more wines which are very different in flavour, and you can make that obvious by choosing two different colours or densities of wine.

Thanks to Dr. Noble's dedication to providing a visual aid to make wine accessible to everyone, it is very easy to use - simply follow the below - but don't forget your wheel:

- Pour yourself a very small glass. To really get the full suite of aromas you need a lot of room left in there, so just under a quarter of a standard glass is plenty. You'll get to top it up once the aroma detecting is over.
- Get swirling it in the glass with your palm pressed gently over the mouth of the glass (and maybe your own) to catch any spills
- Put your nose as deep as you need into the glass and take a deep nasal inhale. Think about the aroma that first comes to mind and then look at your aroma wheel while going with instinct of the immediate hit

- Starting at the bullseye centre of the wheel, look for the aroma that most matches what you can smell. Once you've decided which primary flavour comes to mind, then follow the wheel inwards to start breaking down the flavours even further. If you think it's fruity, you can follow the wheel to decide if it's broken down by tropical fruit / stone fruit / a berry, etc. Follow the wheel to the outer tier for the final level of detail. For example, does it taste like blackberries or raspberries if a berry?
- Write all of these aromas down
- Next, take a bigger sip of wine, holding the wine in your mouth for a second or two, before swallowing. You will probably taste new flavours with this different process and larger mouthful, so repeat the process of following the wheel to find a word that best describes these new flavours.
- Keep tasting and smelling, while writing down each word that comes to mind. Be open to these changes or the words being variable. Then look at your list — these are the words you would use to describe the wine to another expert, which yes we are now calling you.

(Usual Wines, 2020)

It is very easy to train our noses and our brains to connect and quickly identify the aromas in wines, so be confident in having a go and if it makes you feel more comfortable then do this with a close loved-on or on your own if feeling shy (or you are Bridget Jones)

The fastest training tip is to make physical standards to illustrate important and major notes in wine aroma. *(Wine Aroma Wheel, 2020)*

Common aromas and flavours you will see on the Wine Aroma Wheel, and which will appear most commonly at our level, include:

Fruits:

- Blackcurrant
- Apple
- Pear
- Raspberry

Spices:

- Anise
- Black pepper
- Nutmeg

Florals:

- Orange blossom
- Geranium
- Violet

Vegetables:

- Green pepper
- Green almond
- Pepper

Suggested flavours of long ageing:

- Nuts
- Tobacco
- Licorice
- Coffee

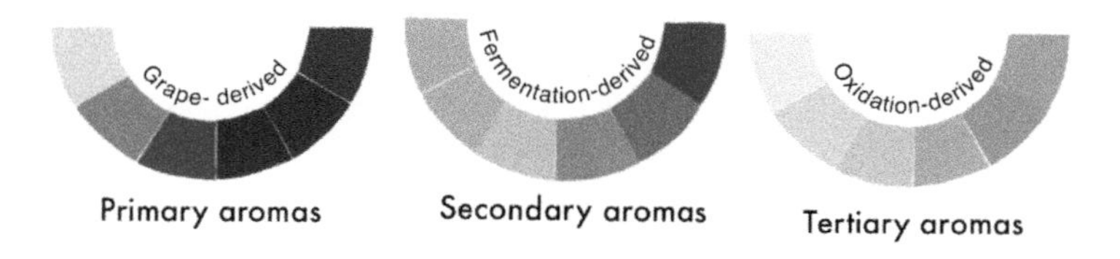

Fig 5. Origin of Wine Aromas

Because wine has such a diverse aroma profile, we advise you to repeat the process several times and enjoy the art of learning aromas and changing detections each time.

To briefly explain what is covered by the above diagram; it helps visualise the levels at which aromas present themselves, and therefore the order in which we tend to identify, and therefore explain, aromas in wines:

- *Primary aromas* are from the type of the grape or the environment in which they grow - for example, Barbera wines will often exhibit subtle nuances of licorice and anise. The range of flavours in the Primary Aroma group include fruit, herbs, earthiness, floral notes, and spices.
- *Secondary Aromas* come from the fermentation process, and include yeast and other microbes. A great example of this is the sour smell that you can find in sparklings that is sometimes described as "yeasty." A general rule is that young wines tend to have more Secondary Aromas than aged wines.
- *Tertiary aromas* (classically referred to as "bouquets") come from ageing wines' oxidation and resting the wine in oak or bottles for extended time. Flavours include vanilla; nutty flavours such as hazelnut in vintages; and dried fruit aromas in older red wines.

(Wine Folly, 2020)

In addition, "faults" in this scenario refers to an excess of any of these flavours, but it is arguable in the wine industry if this is a fair terminology.

The wine aroma wheel, and an understanding of the above aroma levels, gives us all a comprehensible way to describe and compare different wine varietals.

Enjoy this practice and it's easy to use even if you're sparking your love of wine knowledge. Make sure you have one handy for your next dinner party and do something a bit different with a group of friends.

SUMMARY OF DAY 2

Today we have learnt that, much like everything worth knowing in life, wine has a system that takes some getting your head around. We have reviewed the four main categories of Italian wine label classifications, and what they mean; ranging from the highest quality (i.e. highest classification) to the lowest. Namely, the four categories to take away from today are:

- DOCG; or 'Denominazione di Origine Controllata e Garantita' - the highest quality level of wine, created in 1980 in response to criticisms that there were too many DOCs and their quality was variable. There are now 74 DOCG wines in Italy, most of them concentrated in the regions we have covered today, of Piemonte, Tuscany and Veneto. *(Masterclass, 2021)*

- The next level is DOC; or 'Denominazione di Origine Controllata' which translates as "designation of controlled origin." As we covered today, these are mostly outstanding wines, produced in their hundreds in Italy, and which cover many types including sparkling, reds and whites across the country. Remember that each DOC has its own rules about grape varieties, harvest yields and ageing requirements, hence spending time on this designation in particular. *(Masterclass, 2021)*
- Below that, is the huge category of IGT wines; or 'Indicazione Geografica Tipica.' We learned that this is the broadest category and what you will now spot most commonly in the supermarket aisles. The grapes in IGT wines should all come from the IGT region stated on the label, but otherwise the wines do not have to conform to strict classification standards and rules. It doesn't mean there aren't still some

absolute gems in this bracket, they may just not want to stick to the rules.

- And finally, the group which I will refer to in this book for the sake of consistency, as 'Vini Varietali' - otherwise known as wine without a geographical indication and sometimes known as Vino da Tavola or 'table wine' - but with my translation more means a 'generic' wine.

I am all for not being snobby about these things, but theoretically this set of wines are made from grapes grown anywhere in Italy and with no rules of grape combinations etc, so rarely bottled for the European market or exported to the USA. You will more likely find them in a little Italian bar for 6 Euros a bottle if you're lucky enough to visit. *(Masterclass, 2021)*

Today taught us that this system specifies not only the production area and methods for each wine, but also guarantees the quality standard of certain wines which pass a government taste test - with this knowledge, what, and if, you choose to drink from now on, is entirely up to you. Now that you have the classification groups defined, you are armed with the knowledge needed to look more closely at production and the grape families involved.

Finally, today I covered the Wine Aroma Wheel and its purpose - also designed to help you easily identify different aromas in the wines we discuss within this book as a practice, with the help of a colour-coded visual diagram provided above.

Wine aromas are moderately complex, much like the system of classifying them, and from here I leave you with the tools at least, to start detecting some of the several hundred aroma compounds within a single glass of wine. Onwards…

DAY 2 WINE

Our wine on Day 2 as we sail through this glorious week together, is Elibaria Vermentino di Gallura DOCG - a crisp, immediate white wine from family-owned grapevines, grown to reach a state of perfect ripeness.

These aren't just any grapes; they are the Italian island of Sardinia's finest - grown by the Contini family in vineyards located over 200 metres above sea level. *(Svinando, 2020)*

The climate in this area is typically Mediterranean, and as you would expect is characterised by mild winters and warm summers leading to the perfect ripeness Vermentino is celebrated for.

We will look more into aromas in later chapters, but you would immediately be able to distinguish, with your newly-found nose expertise, the main aromas of fruity floral notes and aromatic herbs.

Vermentino di Gallura is Sardinia's only DOCG appellation, and covers white Vermentino-based wines from a large area at the northern end of the island of Sardinia only.

The wine title held DOC status between 1975 and1996, when it became the island's first DOCG wine. *(Wine Searcher, 2019)*

This DOCG dry white wine is a bright straw-yellow colour with almost a greenish tinge and will look simply divine in one of your well-chosen wine glasses at home - more on that shortly.

Vermentino di Gallura wines are based on the Vermentino grape variety - which must legally account for 95% of wine claiming this label. The final 5% may be made up from other authorised non-aromatic white grape varieties.

As discovered in the definitions section above of what gives a wine a certain classification, the wider Vermentino di Sardegna DOC wine group only stipulates an 85% minimum. Vermentino di Sardegna DOC wines have been harvested since 1988 throughout Sardinia - a full 15 years after most of its counterparts *(Wine-searcher, 2020)* and was the culminating result of quality improvements made in Sardinian Vermentino wine production that led to the DOCG status achieved by today's suggested bottle.

The history of how Vermentino arrived in Sardinia in the first place, is not entirely clear - the variety has clear connections with the northwest of Italy as well as Provence and the Languedoc in France, *(Wine-Searcher, 2020)* where it has been known as Rolle for many centuries.

It is also a key variety on the French island of Corsica, immediately north of Sardinia as a neighbouring island. It has been suggested that Vermentino may be of Spanish origin, the other European wine production powerhouse, even though the variety is little known in Spain today.

If this theory is accurate, then the variety would most likely have arrived via Alghero, Italy - which has had a succession of Spanish rulers over the centuries. *(Wine-Searcher, 2020)*

There is a wide variety of soil types throughout the Vermentino di Sardegna DOC area of Sardinia, with vineyards found on pockets of limestone and marl, and viticultural areas dominated by peaks and valleys.

This wine is potentially a little more expensive than our Day 1 tipple at approximately £22 (US$27) but still very affordable and accessible to buy. A few other Vermentino di Gallura Wines based on similar taste, price and community ratings, include the following:

- Vigne Surrau Sciala, Vermentino di Gallura Superiore DOCG
- Vigne Surrau 'Branu', Vermentino di Gallura DOCG
- Cantina del Vermentino 'Funtanaliras' Oro, Vermentino di Gallura DOCG - slightly cheaper at about £12 (US$15)
- Piero Mancini Vermentino di Gallura DOCG, Sardinia
- Capichera Vign'angena, Vermentino di Gallura DOCG, Italy

What foods to pair it with?

For our now somewhat honed palates, our Day 2 wine retains a floral style balanced by a slightly bitter edge, zingy acidity and a hint of minerality. (*Wine Searcher, 2020*)

It offers a tone of white blossoms on the nose, and the main aromas are fruity and floral, accentuated by aromatic herbs you might place as reminiscent of Sardinia.

As such, it is a wine that only needs to be served chilled to successfully accompany an entire lunch or dinner meal ideally based on fish and you're basically transported to the Mediterranean.

Weightier examples can be an excellent food match for creamy chicken or thicker white-sauced fish dishes, while lighter wines from higher altitude vineyards in this wine group complement all manner of seafood dishes.

DAY 2 TAKE AWAY LESSON; HOW TO POUR THE PERFECT GLASS OF WINE

Today we're ready to learn how to pour the optimal glass of wine; i.e. how to hold the bottle (you'd think this part was simple but there's always more to it) and how much wine should be poured - this part is for professionalism-appearance only, if you need a tanker after a long day, you need a tanker.

But in normal circumstances, if you pair this knowledge with what you have learnt in our previous chapter on how to open the bottle correctly, I have every hope you'll be well on your way to properly handling a wine serving – you'll definitely be ahead of the crowd even by this point, when it comes to selecting, pouring and savouring the perfect glass of vino.

I won't go too much into glassware here as your chosen kitchen utensils are really a whole other minefield, but as a basic tip, have a quick look at why certain wine glass shapes are better for certain types of wine, and use this knowledge to find the best few glass shapes or varieties to suit your home collection and lifestyle.

I am certainly not suggesting you need all of them, and two or three of the below types will be plenty for even the most refined of hosts.

Fig 6. Selecting Wine Glasses

So now we've chosen a proper wine glass, there is also an art to getting the right temperature before even thinking about pouring it.

The overall rule to remember is that wine tastes better served slightly cool.

Also, some of the more delicate floral aromatics in fine wines are completely subdued at overly cool temperatures or burn off too quickly when the wine is too warm. *(Wine Folly, 2020)* So in these cases especially, it really is a case of needing to get that sweet spot, rather than just overly-fancy preparation.

A helpful summary of temperatures is below, while not getting too much into the detail here:

- Red Wine: tastes better when served slightly below room temperature from 53 – 69°F (12.5 – 15.5°C) (light red wines like a Pinot Noir taste better at the cooler end of that spectrum and should be served slightly colder)
- White Wine: tastes better from about 44 – 57°F (7.5 – 12°C) (as we get to the oak-aged white wines then the warm side of that spectrum hits the mark)
- Sparkling Wine: The type of Italian sparkling wines we will look at in this book, do great at

about 38 – 45°F (3.5 – 7.5°C) (serve high-quality Champagne and sparkling wines at white wine temperatures instead)

(Wine Folly, 2020)

Now we have the above tips aligned, on how to chill it in advance and have the right wine glass ready, we should now be at the glorious stage of being ready to hear the splash of a perfectly chilled wine hitting our glasses.

Now to pour the perfect glass:

- Firstly, nearly all red wine will taste better decanted; so pour the bottle into a glass pitcher or wine decanter about 30-45 minutes before serving. (The faster way is to use a wine aerator which decants wine almost instantly)
- Pick up the wine bottle from the base and pour directly into the glass, confidently stopping when you have poured a sufficient amount; all in one swift motion. Be bold here!
- To avoid drips, rotate the bottle up and away from you as you lift it away from the glass.
- Pour a standard serving - it is there for a reason! Nobody is saying you can't have more than one glass, but a typical wine glass is 17-25

oz. and designed to hold aroma.(If in doubt, pour to the widest part of the glass - unless using a flute)

- Always hold a wine glass by the stem once poured - your hands will heat up your wine, so not by the bowl, however tempted you might be to grip it for dear life.
- Swirl your glass (orbital swirling) - it draws in oxygen from the air and intensifies the aromas of the wine. If you fill the glass too high, it's difficult to swirl the wine which stops it from being able to breathe *(Bodegas Piqueras, 2022)*
- Then, with any leftovers, store open wines in the fridge - or a wine fridge if you have one, even better.. this slows down any development of the wine, keeping it fresher for longer.

DAY 2 GLOSSARY OF TERMS:

The sotto-zone - subzone

Topograhy - in a wine scenario covers altitude, proximity to hills, inclined land portions, or areas close to bodies of water, as well as the effect these elements has on the grapes and wine

Classico – classic, often used in reference to a historic wine region or a traditional style

Superiore – superior; a wine of a somewhat higher standard —most commonly slightly riper grapes

Riserva – reserve; a wine of longer ageing and usually higher quality

Oenologist - Oenology is the science and study of wine and winemaking

DAY 3

ITALY'S WINE REGIONS

Now on Day 3, we are ready to learn about the Italian Wine Regions in more detail and walk through a detailed wine map of Italy - the regions themselves; the dominant styles of wines produced there and a general understanding of the grapes used.

Also, we will find out the best wines in each region and those which are known for flying the flag for very specific labels. (subject to personal taste on the 'best' part but based on classifications and ratings)

A basic list of the 20 wine regions is below, and we will cover a selection of these that stand out for specific characteristics:

1. Piedmont
2. Tuscany
3. Veneto
4. Emilia-Romagna
5. Lombardy
6. Sicily
7. Abruzzo
8. Trentino Alto-Adige
9. Campania
10. Puglia
11. Friuli-Venezia Giulia
12. Sardinia
13. Marche
14. Lazio
15. Umbria
16. Calabria
17. Molise
18. Basilicata
19. Liguria
20. Aosta Valley

Fig 7. The Regions of Italy

Home to the above 20 separate and distinguishable regions, Italy has a rich and diverse range of both grape varieties and wines spanning the country's landscapes.

Italy's divide into these 20 administrative regions, can be divided even further into several wine sub-regions. The most 'significant' regions, with both quality and quantity taken into consideration, are Piedmonte, Tuscany and Veneto - but we will look beyond just these into the flagship wine styles of the lesser-known regions and their consistently high quality wines. *(Wine-Searcher, 2022)*

THE WINE REGIONS OF NORTHERN ITALY

I have colour-coded the above diagram to give a distinct boundary between the larger areas we refer to these regions sitting *within* - i.e. more broadly as Northern, Central and Southern Italy. This is a helpful initial understanding of the Italy map (here's me giving geography advice) before breaking it down even further into regions.. so everyone refresh their compass skills please as it's thankfully that simple so far. The below is what we count as Northern Italy therefore:

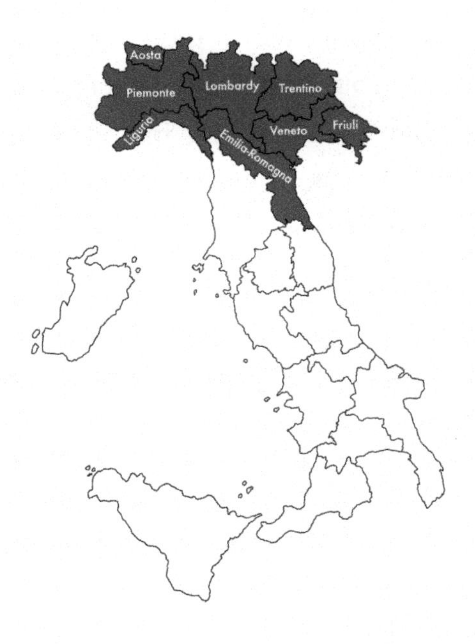

Fig 8. Northern Italy Regions

The part of North Italy attached to Europe with the Alps and the Apennines, is a mountainous climate that is mostly cold and then mild summers.

Vineyards range from sea level in eastern Emilia-Romagna to around 4,200 ft above sea level in the mineral-rich Aosta Valley. *(Italy Foodies, 2020)*

Valle d'Aosta

This historic, autonomous region of Valle d'Aosta (Aosta Valley to you and I) produces high-quality grapes in exclusive micro-zones, in the Northwestern corner of Italy. It is the smallest wine region in the country by size but produces everything from rich Petit Rouge, Fumin, and Vien de Nus used to create spicy wines, to Petite Arvine (a white grape similar to Pinot Grigio) used to make fruity whites. *(Italy Foodies, 2020)*

The Aosta Valley is home to more than 20 unique wines, including Pinot Noir rosé and other regional wines completely specific to the region, such as:

- Arnad Montjove
- Blanc de Morgex
- Donnas.

The valley created perfect conditions for late-ripening Nebbiolo grapes that take on the flavour of the soil they are grown in, to produce powerful blends and a fruity aroma.

Most of the more classic wines of the region, such as the much-beloved dinner party favourite Pinot Grigio, retain both floral and citrus notes. *(Italy Foodies, 2020)*

Alpine Trentino and Valle d'Aosta (Aosta Valley again to you and I) are similar to one another, although wine production in the Aosta Valley is a mere 2.1 million litres annually *(Wine Searcher, 2020)*, with cultural and winemaking influences from across the border in Austria and Switzerland boasting an almost cult-following, which we will look at in more detail in a later Chapter when looking at wine trends emerging in Italy and beyond.

As mentioned earlier, there are a few regions within each of these broad areas of Italy that stand out purely for flagship wines or the sheer quantity of a label produced there, and in the case of Northern Italy, Piemonte takes the title.

Piemonte is home to many of the wine labels you may know and love already, even if new to studying Italian wine at this (hopefully not tediously overcommitted) level; including Barolo, Barbaresco and Moscato d'Asti, among many others.

So let's now look at this famous region a bit more closely, and hey, while we're at i,t maybe book a holiday there as well.

Piemonte

Known as Piedmont in English but one of the ones I feel needs to be spelt in its native tongue, Piemonte delivers a vast range of wine styles and is one of Italy's most acclaimed wine growing regions, while ranked 6th in highest production volume. *(Wine Folly, 2020)*

Maybe it is even more well-known for its notably high-quality wine and the fact that it produces more DOCG wines than any other region.

In Piemonte, there are a total of 59 sub-regions, including Barolo, Gabiano, Barbera and many of the names you will be starting to recognise.

The name of the region is listed prominently on Piemonte wine labels and then noted alongside the variety. *(Wine-Searcher, 2019)*

Barbera is the most planted variety in Piemonte *(Wine Folly, 2020)*, and it is this you'll often find the locals drinking, so read on if you want to mimic the glorious curbside culture of an Italian holiday destination in your garden during a soggy barbeque.

The great wines of Barbera deliver aromas of red and black berries, espresso, fresh anise, velvety tannins and a spicy finish. The wines are often oaked specifically for these richer fruit flavours, but most everyday Barbera you will find are medium-bodied with a hint of spicy-earth terroir. *(Wine Folly, 2020)*

After trying several of these wines, the really high-quality ones we personally recommend you to try from Piemonte are as below:

- Barbera d'Asti Sottozona "Nizza" DOCG
- Piemonte Barbera DOC

Veneto

The region of Veneto produces a vast output of wine; in 2021 it made over one billion litres. *(Wine Searcher, 2020)* In case you're not already planning to move there immediately based on that alone, it also produces one of the world's richest, finest wines which we will look at more closely shortly, as a flagship of Italian wine-making - Amarone della Valpolicella.

The most popular wines, as well as the above, is Prosecco, (the sparkling gem which we will give deserved time to properly later on, made by the Glera grape) and Soave *(Vino Vest, 2020)*

Thanks to these names and the volume of wine produced here, Veneto is one of the most important of the Italian wine regions, and one whose grapes we will look at more closely in the next chapter.

While not as large as most of the other wine regions, it produces more wine proportionately than any other region and also many styles. *(Vintage Roots, 2016)*

In terms of a cracking Prosecco, our favourite is the Giol Prosecco Vino Spumante - but a few of our other favourite wines from the Veneto region include the below:

- Fasoli Gino DOC Soave Borgoletto; a flowery wine with full aromatic flavours
- Fasoli Gino DOCG Amarone La Corte del Pozzo; a strong wine of liquorice, blackcurrant and spice flavours
- Fasoli Gino DOC Soave Borgoletto; an unoaked, flowery white wine

Other international varieties you are likely to know already from this region include the much-loved Cabernet Sauvignon and Pinot Noir.

Friuli-Venezia Giulia

In the very far northeast, Friuli-Venezia Giulia marks not only the somewhat blurred boundary between Italy with Slovenia and Austria but is also home to a high-quality wine industry alongside a more cult, minimal intervention wine scene in the likes of Collio Goriziano near the border. *(Vino Vest, 2020)*

Often just referred to as 'Collio,' Collio Goriziano is a wine DOC covering the hills around Gorizia, Friuli-Venezia Giulia, and known for its complex, aromatic Collio Bianco - a white wine put firmly on the Italian wine map in the 1970s and 80s thanks to its aroma and purity of fruit. *(Vino Vest, 2020)*

This is just one stand-out white wine of the region, arguably the king of white-wine Italian regions (huge statement), with over 75% of white grapes; the highest share in the country.

Within it, there are over 30 different grapes, including several of the best-known names we all love, including the smaller share of its reds - Sauvignon Blanc, Riesling, Pinot Grigio, Chardonnay, Pinot Noir, Cabernet Sauvignon and Merlot among others.

Known also for its distillates and traditional grape-based brandy, Friuli-Venezia Giulia is home to grape varieties of note, including Tocai Friulano and Ribolla used for the region's signature white wines above, as well as Malvasia, Glera and Prosecco. *(Italy Foodies, 2020)*

Classified wines produced here include four DOCGs, twelve DOCs and three IGPs,

Although Liguria of Northern Italy appears to have all the interesting grape varieties, it remains rarely seen outside of its domestic market and is one to look for when travelling in Italy for its unique accessibility in Italy alone.

Known as the Italian Riviera, its steep hills by the Mediterranean sea make vine-growing challenging, resulting in scattered planting with limited production - some only reachable by boat. So, one for a stunning holiday and Insta-perfect photo opportunity clutching a local wine.

Further inland, the hillsides offer only marginally less daunting vertical slopes, and so the planting of vines is dense and compact as well as tricky; but viticulture plays an essential role in the prevention of soil erosion and landslides. (*Wine Searcher, 2020*)

Despite the harsh environment, vines have been grown in this area for more than 25 centuries, and later in Roman times, the most famous area to emerge was the even more Insta-perfect Cinque Terre (meaning *Five Lands* to us), now a DOC/DOP wine area in the far east of the region near La Spezia. (*Wine Searcher, 2020*)

Emilia-Romagna, meanwhile, was once only known for the then-favoured Lambrusco sparkling wines, despite a range of wines worthy of greater attention which we will look at briefly below.

Emilia Romagna

Emilia Romagna is Italy's agricultural hub and one of the most fertile regions in the country. Add to this the food produced there; it is also considered Italy's capital of gastronomy, which for a foodie country we know is no small flag to bear.

It is famous for producing cured meats like prosciutto hams, aged cheeses such as Parmigiano-Reggiano and sauces such as balsamic vinegar.

In contrast to the rich foods produced there, the wines produced are light and famously slightly sparkling, otherwise known as "frizzante' which we will refer to from here — a perfect pairing of food to wine.

Varieties found here include:

- Adaptive Trebbiano
- Barbera
- Gutturnio (produced in the hills of Piacenza)
- Lambrusco
- Malvasia
- Sauvignon
- Sangiovese
- Bonarda

(Wine Searcher, 2020)

A large percentage of these grapes are used to produce sparkling wines, either frizzante or spumante, of which the most notable are from the five Lambrusco DOCs as below:

- Salamino di Santa Croce
- Salamino di Sorbara
- Grasparossa di Castelvetra
- Modena
- Reggiano

(Wine Searcher, 2020)

Despite its wide portfolio of well-known Italian and international varieties, Emilia-Romagna's unique charm and what you should try if you get to visit, are the rare local DOC wines that you can pluck from small independent vineyards to your hearts' content.

THE WINE REGIONS OF CENTRAL ITALY

Fig 9. Central Italy Regions

Think of everything Italian that you love, and most of it will be found in this central region of the country. Rome, Florence and Pisa's ancient history, buzzing wine bars and packed streets, to Umbria's Medieval towns of Perugia and Assisi.

Central Italy has five wine regions: Marches, Abruzzo, Tuscany, Umbria, and Lazio.

The region is split in the middle by the Apennine Mountains and grapes are grown on either side of the mountain range extending out to the Mediterranean and Adriatic seas.

The coastal influence makes this region perfect for growing two key red grape varieties primarily - Sangiovese and Montepulciano. *(Total Wine, 2020)*

Small towns like Orvieto have their rightful mention on our wine map too, dramatically positioned on a rocky slope and the ideal spot to drink their famously crisp white wine while taking in the views.

In complete contrast, across the Apennines, you can enjoy the ragged, wild beauty of Abruzzo and Molise. offering a refreshing change from the tourist trail. At the centre of all this is Tuscany; one of the best wine regions in Italy if not the world, and a favourite among wine lovers - but all of these regions also do excellent wines specific to their own growing conditions and climate, which we will celebrate here.

Undeniably though, Tuscany truly is Italy's poster child for wine, helped along by its charming rolling hills, terracotta roofs, and stunning vistas. Much-loved by the novice wine lover for its generic Chianti as covered on Day 1 when trying a fine example - for the more refined connoisseur (that includes you now) it is also home to some of the most prestigious and rarer wines we will look at first:

Tuscany

What exactly are the typical terroirs of Tuscany and the production areas that make it such a stand-out area for winemaking? Let's discover all the main wine-growing areas of Tuscany and its labels to look for, from the wines of Central Tuscany to the wines of the Tyrrhenian Coast.

Firstly, Tuscany produces some of Italy's most reputable wines, and a lot of the names you will hear a lot day-to-day for widely produced and very well-known titles; Chianti Classico and Vino Nobile di Montepulciano for example. *(Wine Searcher, 2022)*

It is predominantly a red wine region (mainly Sangiovese) but also produces delicious whites we certainly recommend you to try, such as Vernaccia di San Gimignano and Vin Santo.

Fig 10. Sangiovese wine bottle

The best-known wine-growing areas in this region are the famous Chianti hills, but also the Mugello area, Val di Chiana and the coastal strip. *(Visit Italy, 2020)*

In the region, all the above famous Tuscan Sangiovese-based red wines are produced, including Chianti Classico, Brunello di Montalcino, Nobile di Montepulciano, Carmignano and the historic Tuscan white wine par excellence: Vernaccia di San Gimignano.

Central Tuscany has also given birth to countless prestigious international vines such as Cabernet Sauvignon, Cabernet Franc and Merlot; as well as Syrah, in Cortona and Montecarlo, and Pinot Nero in both Mugello and Casentino. *(Italy's Finest Wines, 2022)*

The most famous Tuscan wines of the Tyrrhenian coastal area are produced in Bolgheri, with all the international varieties you'd have heard of above. Maremma, on the other hand, is the homeland of Morellino di Scansano - a famous Tuscan red wine made from Sangiovese grapes and locally called Morellino.

These, for me, are even more charming finds in an otherwise huge production region and I will do my best to suggest everything from the DOCG wines found here, to charmed local delicacies.

As well as the outstanding red wines from the area, Tuscany celebrates white grape varieties such as Vermentino for example, particularly in Bolgheri and in the territory of Candia dei Colli Apuani, as well as Ansonica in the Maremma and insular Tuscany on the Island of Elba and on the island of Giglio. *(Italy's Finest Wines, 2022)*

The most highly regarded, the region is also home to the below DOCG wines to try:

- Carmignano DOCG
- Il Vino Nobile di Montepulciano DOCG
- Vernaccia di San Gimignano DOCG
- Vino nobile di Montepulciano DOCG

Grape types found in Tuscany include:

- Sangiovese; the major grape used to make Chianti
- Trebbiano; most produced variety for Tuscany's whites
- Cab;
- Merlot, and;
- Vermentino; a range of these varieties produce some of the finest red and white wines available in the region
- Ciliegiolo; a native grape used in the Chianti DOC
- Syrah; producing strong and full-bodied wines.

(Italy Foodies, 2020)

Among the best DOC wines produced in Tuscany includes:

- Bolgheri DOC
- Syrah DOC of Cortona
- Rosso di Montalcino DOC
- Maremma Toscana DOC
- Vin Santo del Chianti Classico DOC

Some notable other Tuscan wine styles to celebrate and try include the below:

- Super Tuscans - such as Tignanello, Masseto, Solaia and Sassicaia, made from Cab and Merlot grapes
- A sweet wine called Vin Santo is a Tuscan specialty but not for those without a sweet tooth and a love of biscotti served on the side

Wineries to visit if you make it there yourself:

If in Tuscany, then 1. Put this book down and enjoy a wine immediately, and 2. Visit the amazing Salcheto Winery in Montepulciano - a unique example of sustainable and off-the-grid winemaking with a wholesome story and well-worth a visit for a winery tour and lunch.

To the south of Central Italy, Umbria and Lazio are probably best known for their once widely-encountered whites - in Umbria this was Orvieto and in Lazio, Frascati.

But both now offer significantly more interest to the curious and learned wine lover, including the excellently-titled Est! Est!! Est!!! di Montefiascone DOC title wine which should maybe be tried for the name alone.

Umbria

Umbria is best known for white wine production, and the signature Orvieto DOC mentioned above, remains the region's largest wine appellation.

It is made from the Trebbiano grape variety, also referred to as Procanico in Umbria, and accounts for over ten percent of the overall region's wine production. *(Wine Searcher, 2019)* Styles of the famous Umbia Orveito can vary from anything from dry, through to semi-sweet or sweet white wines.

Grechetto is the next most prominent white wine variety in the region, playing a supporting role in Orvieto and various other Biancos in the region. But most of the other white wine DOCs here – including Colli Martani and Amelia – also allow for varietal bottlings of Grechetto. *(Wine Searcher, 2019)*

Although best-known for its whites, as is sometimes the case with the classifications, Umbria's two top level DOCG designations are reserved for noteworthy **red** wines which certainly are both worth a mention here.

The native red grape Sagrantino has gained prominence and popularity in the Montefalco area, creating strong wines by producers such as Paolo Bea and Arnaldo Caprai. *(Wine Searcher, 2019)*

Sangiovese is also growing in popularity and is the region's most planted grape variety, red or white. It accounts for around 22 percent of vineyard area and is the principal grape of the second of the region's DOCG wines - both listed below.

(Wine Searcher, 2020)

Umbria's two DOCG wines to try:

- Sagrantino di Montefalco DOCG
- Torgiano Rosso Riserva DOCG

Lazio

Lazio is the region in Central Italy which is home to Italy's capital city of Rome. (Italian and Latin *"Roma"* if we want to continue being polished and European)

Rome is also the capital of the Lazio region, the centre of the Metropolitan City of Rome, as well as a special comune named Comune di Roma Capitale - and located in the central-western portion of the Italian Peninsula on the shores of the Tiber.

The Lazio region's reputation in the wine world is mainly based on its white wines; the main popular grape varieties here being Trebbiano, Malvasia di Candia and Malvasia Puntinata. *(Wine Searcher, 2019)* The modern-day styles of these crisp whites are lighter and drier thanks to modern vinification methods. *(Wine Searcher, 2019)*

However, they are still designed for drinking young, (the wines, not us - don't panic) i.e. not aged for long and characterised by their sharpness, acidity and a light freshness that suits food pairing to the local Lazio cuisine. *(Wine Searcher, 2019)* Lazio speciality dishes include porchetta; a succulent pork roasted with herbs, and abbacchio; a young lamb - both of which are complemented by a wine that cuts through the heaviness.

Although Lazio's red wines are not as high profile, they are beginning to make a serious name for themselves. This is especially true for those made from Sangiovese, Cesanese, Montepulciano, Merlot and Nero Buono di

Coro grapes *(Wine Searcher, 2019)* which we have seen successfully cultivated in other regions.

There are more than 200 grape varieties in the area, and it is home to 27 DOC titles representing a hugely varied collection of wines. Three white DOCs probably stand out in terms of profile, listed below:

- Frascati;
- Castelli Romani - an appellation based on the above, and;
- The aforementioned Est! Est!! Est!!! di Montefiascone, which is produced around Lake Bolsena

(Wine Searcher, 2019)

Special designations of Frascati represent two of Lazio's three top-level DOCG wines, both credited in 2011:

- Frascati Superiore designation (for dry white wines)
- Cannelino di Frascati, for sweet wines only

The third Lazio DOCG is:

- Cesanese del Piglio; whose leading red wine is Velletri, a robust wine made from Sangiovese, Cesanese, Montepulciano, Merlot and Ciliegiolo; also produced as a riserva.

The Roma DOC was set up in 2011 to provide a familiar and united marketable name for producers around the city of Rome. *(Wine Searcher, 2019)*

It also overlaps many other Lazio DOCs fully or partially, and although not frequently used for Frascati, producers in lesser-known locations in Lazio might use the capital's name and you will see this on their bottles.

Lazio IGP designation is the one most commonly seen on wine labels - applying to the less stringent classified wines we covered earlier and that you will see frequently across Europe. Some of these are still excellent wines even if the regulations are more flexible, and a recommended variety is the Spanish Tempranillo.

Some excellent vino da tavola is also being made here such as the Bordeaux Kings Cabernet Sauvignon and Merlot Compete, as well as versions of this in partnership with the local Cesanese. *(Wine Searcher, 2019)*

On the other side of the Apennines to Lazio, the regions of Marche and Abruzzo face the Adriatic and boast as much picturesque scenery as Tuscany. The Marche's flagship wines are undoubtedly the herbaceous and nutty whites of Verdicchio dei Castelli di Jesi, and others we will look at more closely below.

Marche

Marche is a region on the eastern side of Central Italy and predominantly another region in this part of the country associated with white wines over red, namely from the Trebbiano and Verdicchio grape varieties, where Marche has been home for more than 600 years. (*Wine-Searcher, 2019*)

Its winemaking heritage spans thousands of years, similarly to the other primary wine regions of Italy, and has been influenced by the Etruscans, Romans and Lombards we studied in the introduction. Its long history and impact of these cultures explains the breadth of vinicultural tradition and wine styles in the region, and as such it also produces fewer, but still notable, high-quality reds that we will look at here (it's only fair.)

Marche occupies the triangular area you will see in the above picture, bordered by the Adriatic Sea on the East, and neighboured by Emilia-Romagna and Abruzzo regions to the North and South and separated from Umbria by the Apennines. *(Wine-Searcher, 2019)*

The influence of its position means various climates create both warm and cool viticultural zones within the region. Vineyards cover around 25,000 hectares and produce almost two million hectoliters of wine annually.

The majority of this is sold as Vino di Tavola or under the IGT Marche classification we looked at on Day 2 which means it is lower classification standards. Marche has 20% of wines sold under the region's fifteen DOC and four DOCG wine titles, *(Wine-Searcher, 2019)* all of which rightfully deserve their title.

The finest expressions of Verdicchio we believe, are found in the DOCGs listed below:

- Verdicchio dei Castelli di Jesi
- Verdicchio di Matelica

Another notable white wine from Marche that is well worth a try in our experience is:

- Bianchello del Metauro

Among the smaller collection of red wines from Marche, the finest are generally Montepulciano and /

or Sangiovese, and I would highly recommend the below:

- Rosso Conero Riserva
- Ciliegiolo
- Terreni di Sanseverino
- Lacrima di Morro d'Alba

Abruzzo

Neighbouring region, Abruzzo, is another central Italian wine region that can't be overlooked, sitting on the East (Adriatic) coast. Its immediate neighbours include Lazio to the West and South-West, and Molise to the South-East. The stand-out grape varieties of Abrusso are the native red Montepulciano and white Trebbiano, both the poster-childs for wines in the area.

There are also a few international varieties playing a part in Abruzzo, such as Chardonnay, Cabernet Sauvignon and Merlot, *(Wine-Searcher, 2019)* as well as more commonly-found native varieties we have seen a lot of in other regions, such as Sangiovese.

The usual maturation process for Abruzzo wine is in oak, but the famed Montepulciano Cerasuolo is aged in stainless steel and a stand-out flagship must-try of the regions' DOC wines.

Abruzzo is home to three DOC wine designations; the red and Cerasuolo d'Abruzzo and the aforementioned Montepulciano d'Abruzzo, as well as thirdly - the white wine appellation Trebbiano d'Abruzzo. At the highest classification, it is home to only one (but rather splendid) DOCG wine;

- Montepulciano d'Abruzzo Colline Teramane DOCG

Winemaking traditions in Abruzzo date back to the sixth century BC and the Etruscans we met in the introduction, played a major role in introducing viniculture to the area as well as many others in Italy. At the time Abruzzo's vineyards were generally focused around the Peligna valley in the province of L'Aquila. *(Wine-Searcher, 2019)* Sadly in later years, viniculture was sidelined for many centuries as the Abruzzo region's population went into decline. *(Wine-Searcher, 2019)*

The last 40-50 years since the resurgence of the 1960's new era of wine-making have seen a true renaissance in winemaking in this region in particular, thanks in part to a truly heartwarming effort by co-operative wineries in the Chieti province to turn it around. *(Wine-Searcher, 2019)*

Historically a poor area, Abruzzo is now flourishing and continually gaining economic ground as well as its rightful reputation in great wines to celebrate.

It is not on par in terms of production with many of the other Central Italian wine regions, but I am keen to show you some of these areas as well and give you different perspectives with which you look at Italian wine.

The main importers of Abruzzo wine are Germany, the USA and Canada *(Wine-Searcher, 2019)* - so if reading from there you may find yourself more closely connected to this understated wine region than you thought.

Volumes heading to the UK, Sweden, Denmark and Norway are also on the rise and we look forward to supporting their exports. After all, Abruzzo has at least 36,000 hectares of land dedicated to vines and an annual production of more than 350 million litres - now Italy's fifth most prominent wine region after Sicily, Puglia, Veneto and Emilia-Romagna. *(Wine Searcher, 2019)*

Excitingly, we leave Central Italy with a new age of wineries gearing towards producing more quality-driven wines - with a notable increase in recent years of sustainable and boutique wineries. More to follow on Day 7. *(Wine Searcher, 2019)*

THE WINE REGIONS OF SOUTHERN ITALY

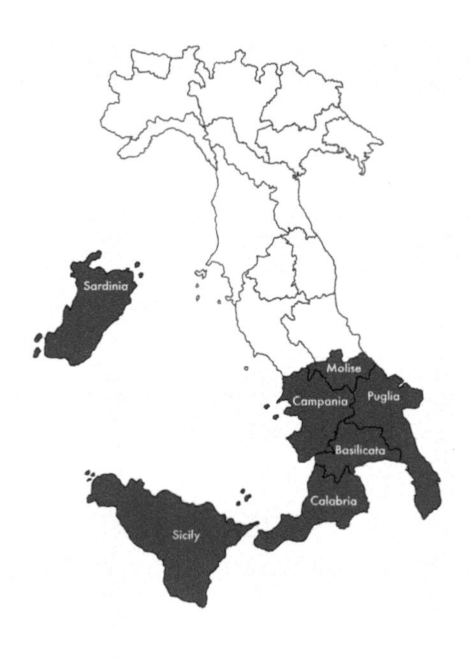

Fig 11. Southern Regions of Italy

Just to the South of Abruzzo sits the tiny, hilly region of Molise and working our way down from there onwards, we are now in what we classify as Southern Italy - yes that's right, we're in Italy's 'heel' (well, almost.)

This far South and the Italian wines owe much to the ancient connections to Greece and the Balkans from generations prior, continuing to produce deep, tannic and flavourful red wines, spanning Campania, the Gaglioppos of Calabria, the Negroamaros and Puglia. *(Italy Foodies, 2020)*

Molise

Molise is part of a partly untouched Southern Italian region that is historic, rustic and archaeological while bearing traces of seasonal migration of communities and widespread livestock.

Wines produced in this small gem of a region include a recent DOC classification of Biferno wines (red, white, and rosé) which are crisp and acidic, as well as its Pentro di Isernia wines (Italy Foodies, 2020) which come from the dominant grape varieties found here - Trebbiao, Montepulciano and Aglianico which we will cover in more detail tomorrow. *(Italy Foodies, 2020)*

Puglia

Puglia is home to picturesque hills, vast plains and the Mediterranean Sea coastline. Thanks to a recent resurgence in its popularity, which I support entirely but seems an entirely random social media phenomenon, it has cemented its place in the ranks of Italy's famous holiday destinations and something of a phenomenon.

As a wine region, it has everything the holidaymaker is seeking as well in abundance: ancient towns heavy with their history and producing excellent gastronomy experiences, and a freedom from the the crowds of Campania and Tuscany. *(Lonely Planet, 2022)*

Puglia can be divided into three rough viticultural areas, which conveniently for you and I, correspond to its administrative wine provinces: Foggia in the North, Bari and Taranto in the middle and Brindisi and Lecce in the South of the region. *(Wine Searcher, 2020)*

Fig 12. Puglia

The Southern half of the Puglian region is of great significance to Puglia's identity in comparison to the North, and is almost entirely flat - retaining a strong connection with its Greco-Roman past and not joining the practises of the Central Italy popularised wine-making trends. *(Wine Searcher, 2020)*

The wines are slightly different between the North and South of the region too, but they are united by one factor - the choice of crops grown: olives and grapes respectively. The region is responsible for almost half of Italy's total olive-oil production and has a long-held reputation as a prolific source of (majoritively red) wine. *(Wine Searcher, 2020)*

But as the world began to demand higher-quality wines and became interested in the supply chain, the mass-produced blending wines in which Puglia specialised lost their value.

Consumers today demand quality over quantity – and at the turn of the century Puglia began to reduce the loose yield restrictions imposed under its DOC regulations, and to change its approach completely to winemaking. *(Wine Searcher, 2020)*

At that point in history only a tiny percentage of Puglian wine was of DOC quality, and it has taken a while for the region to cover from its approach of mass production and embrace the classification system.

The high quality classified wines are now climbing steadily and it is interesting to look at the region as one that has had to adopt change and move with the times to retain its position in the wine world. New DOCs are being introduced consistently, and in 2010 the region gained its first DOCG in Primitivo di Manduria Dolce Naturale, followed a year later by a trio of red wines lifted up out of the Castel del Monte DOC. *(Wine*

Searcher, 2020) Currently the region holds six IGT titles and just over 30 DOC titles.

Puglia is also a land of fruity well-valued wine - classified across the world as formidable and supreme, to be tried at their finest while sipping it from an authentic Puglian bar at sunset ideally. The titles to try are as follows:

- Primitivo di Manduria
- Negroamaro
- Salice Salentino
- Castel Del Monte Aglianico

(Italy Foodies, 2020)

Grapes found in the region include: spiced Negroamaro and Primitivo; known for producing tannic wines and; Verdeca, a rare white-wine grape which we will look at in more detail tomorrow. In closing on this stunning region, I must reiterate once again that if planning an 'off the beaten track' visit to Puglia as a wine tour in-person, then the "true" Puglia is said to be found in the Southernmost stretch of the Appian Way - where the wines are made from grape varieties almost unique to the area. This is where you will see the true charm of Puglian wine, while in the North as mentioned above, the prevalent grapes are those used all over Central and Northern Italy (such as Sangiovese and Montepulciano) - sure you will still try some delicious wine, but head South for variety.

Sicily

Sicily is defined by its natural beauty; an island of mountains, stretches of beaches and historic monuments. Much of Sicily's food is seafood and fish orientated, and gastronomers flock here for the authentic seafood cuisine. *(Italy Foodies, 2020)*

Fig 13. The Island of Sicily

The wines found in the region pay homage to this and pair perfectly with local dishes - here, the Nero d'Avola reigns over the wine scene, despite Sicily boasting a fine selection including Frappato, Nerello Mascalese and Zibibbo.

Grapes found in Sicily include:

- Trebbiano
- Syrah
- Chardonnay, and;
- Nero d'Avola - a native grape.

Wines produced here include:

- Nero D'Avola - most famously, originating in South-East Sicily
- Alcamo;
- Moscato di Noto, and;
- Fortified wines like Marsala - all produced around Mt Etna.

And lastly while in Southern Italy, a look at the wine production on the stunning island of Sardinia:

Sardinia

Sardinia sits to the west of the country as a crossroads of Mediterranean influences off the coast of mainland

Italy, and is the second-largest island in the Mediterranean Sea.

It is almost three times the size of the French island of Corsica, its neighbouring island to the North, and only marginally smaller than Italy's other major island of Sicily. *(Wine Searcher, 2019)*

Fig 14. The Island of Sardinia

The island has belonged to various empires and kingdoms over the centuries, and these unique influences are reflected in everything from its architecture, languages and dialects, to its unique portfolio of wine grapes and production.

The separate identity to the mainland has led to a difference in the Sardinian relationship with wine versus mainlanders. Wine is less culturally ingrained here than in the mainland regions of Italy, perhaps due to the changeable history and its rulers, and as such its wine production and consumption has only truly developed in the past few centuries. *(Wine Searcher, 2019)*

Making up for lost time, in that time Sardinia now has more DOC and IGT titles than Calabria and Basilicata combined, despite having the lowest wine production per hectare of any Italian wine region *(Wine Searcher, 2019)* - but this shows a penchant for lower classified wines that have been through less rigorous standard controls and reflects that in reality, viticulture is still a minority enterprise in Sardinia, despite generous financial incentives from the government. *(Wine Searcher, 2019)*

Only a small percentage of the island's land is given over to vineyards, and perhaps versus easier capitalisation on tourism for the locals, there seems to be little drive to capitalise on the island's wine friendly landscape.

Fortunately, Sardinia is another region in which there is a story developing of a new age for winemaking; a handful of producers have begun creating high-quality wines and now gaining the international recognition they deserve.

The location specific DOC wines line the West Coast, and are a strip of excellent varieties - running from South to North:

- Carignano del Sulcis
- Vernaccia di Oristano
- Malvasia di Bosa and;
- Alghero. *(Wine Searcher, 2019)*

Sardinia's only DOCG wine is Vermentino di Gallura, unusually for the newly acclaimed quality wines, harvested in the far North - Eastern corner. However the most familiar appellations to many drinkers are likely to be the island-wide DOCs Cannonau di Sardegna and Vermentino di Sardegna, a name you are more likely to have seen imported into our supermarkets and still deserving of trying.

We have reached the end of selection of Italy's wine regions, and those of the 20 we have not covered, we will look at instead tomorrow when studying the native grape varieties of regions. The idea is to give you an understanding of the types of wines produced in various climates of the different areas of the country, and choose from the mainstream flagship areas as well as the smaller regions with far smaller production numbers, to consider the whole range of production in the country. As if you hadn't already heard enough about grape varieties my friends, it's on to Day 4.

SUMMARY OF DAY 3

So, today we have looked at the 20 administrative regions of Italy - all of which produce wines worth learning at least a little about, and many of which we have delved deeper into, in terms of the wines grown and grape regions within them. The most 'significant,' if putting a label on it (pardon the pun) for sheer quality and quantity delivered, are commonly understood to be Tuscany, Piedmont and Veneto *(Wine Searcher, 2019)* - where we spent some time learning about their climates and outputs.

I have covered how each region has its flagship wine styles, and recommended those which stand out as excellent quality or internationally recognisable varieties to be aware of in the wine world. Some are famous because they are produced in large volumes, such as the above three regions, and can be found all over the world; others because of their consistently high quality *(Wine Searcher, 2019)* and timeless appeal, even if smaller in regional size and harder to come by.

I hope today has given you a sense of Italian traditions of winemaking being unique to its land, its climate and its people.

Whether you're new to the world of wine, a seasoned taster interested in more recommendations or just looking for the right red to pair with your next dinner party, one thing is for sure — nothing beats the selection of Italian wines on offer across the country and its islands.

There's a lifetime of learning that goes into knowing wine and understanding the subtleties and complexities of grapes, making wine, tasting it, and then deciding its quality - we are also still learning every day. I hope today has handed you the basics you will need as a wine lover either looking to expand your knowledge from home, or travelling to Italy to visit a wine region in person.

You are armed with the wines grown from which Italian regions; what grapes to look for and hopefully what kind of wine tour might be right for you. All that remains is if visiting, bring us back a bottle.

DAY 3 WINE

On Day 3 we have a heart-warming family story to celebrate today's chosen bottle (but a far more expensive price point!) to give you an example of the pinnacle of Italian wine you can indulge in when and if ready - Biondi-Sanit Brunello di Montalcino.

This Biond-Santi wine reflects the Tuscan territory it comes from, in its acidity and berry flavours of the hillside vineyards at Il Greppo. The wine is typically elegant, sophisticated and built to age - but the price reflects this and a bottle will set you back about £150 (US$ 180) so it's one to save for a celebration.- we have more affordable alternatives for you to try!

You will see immediately on pouring a glass (properly; aka Day 2's lesson) that the colour is a rich, dark red hue and the aromas are red and black fruit, including black cherry, strawberries, figs and red plums. It also has an underlying hint of vanilla, spices and earthiness. It is full-bodied with alcohol levels around 14 or 15% abv and bright acidity to provide balance. *(Wine Enthusiast, 2022)*

Looking back at its history, Biondi-Sanit Brunello di Montalcino was first created by Ferruccio Biondi Santi in the late 1800s, who established a tradition and methodology that is retained until today by his grandson, Franco Biondi Santi along with the help of his two children. *(Wine Enthusiast, 2020)*

From the family estate at Il Greppo, Brunello's original birthplace, Il Greppo wines set the standard for the entire township and region of Tuscany, and it has directly influenced notable producers such as Castello Banfi, Altesino, Argiano, Capanna and Poggio Antico among many others. *(Wine Enthusiast, 2020)*

The present day Brunello del Greppo now has twenty five hectares dedicated to production and the traditional agronomy and cellaring practices are still used by Franco and his family to give this grape its character and quality. Biondi-Santi harvests early and the wines are subject to a long maceration period, in steel for the Brunello and oak for the Riserva, and are then aged in large oak casks. (Berry Bros & Rudd, 2020)

Other examples of high-end, special occasion Biondi-Santi Montalcinos' to try include:

- 2010 Brunello di Montalcino, Biondi-Santi, Tuscany - approx £120 (US$145) per bottle
- 2016 Rosso di Montalcino, Tenuta Greppo, Biondi-Santi, Tuscany - approx £680 (US$825) for a case of six

More affordable alternatives for everyday:

- 2019 Rosso di Montalcino DOC - approx £17 (US$20)
- 2019 Casanova di neri Rosso di Montalcino DOC- approx £21 (US$25)

Today, the wider wine group of Brunello di Montalcino has over 200 producers that make more than 300 thousand cases per year, *(Wine Insiders, 2022)* and many of these are also excellent and well worth being your 'treat' bottle of red at some stage in your life. However, due to its high quality but low production numbers, it remains one of Italy's most expensive and sought after wines and price points are high from any vineyard.

White DOCG regulations simply stipulate 100% Sangiovese grapes, not all Sangiovese is suited for Brunello wine. The Montalcino region is known for its unique clones of Sangiovese grapes that have adapted specifically to the local terroir. *(Wine Insiders, 2022)*

What foods to pair with?

Due to its high acidity and elegant, rich body, Brunello pairs well with a wide variety of foods - particularly heavy meat dishes such as steak and game, and especially paired with mushroom sauces. It also can bode well against heavy pasta dishes, stews and powerful cheeses. *(Wine Insiders, 2022)*

In contrast, Brunello is not ideal for lighter dishes such as seafood, salad, or poultry and should be matched instead with the rich foods mentioned above. All in all, this is a meal and paired wine you shouldn't save for your tightest jeans.

Other examples of (more affordable) Brunello di Montalcino to try: *(Decanter, 2022)*

- Padelletti, Brunello di Montalcino, Tuscany
- Val di Suga, Brunello di Montalcino, Tuscany
- Canalicchio Franco Pacenti, Brunello di Montalcino, Tuscany
- Cortonesi, La Mannella, Brunello di Montalcino, 2017

(All in the £35 - £50 bracket)

DAY 3 TAKE AWAY LESSON; HOW TO READ ITALIAN WINE LABELS

We know from Day 2 that wine classification, and therefore what's on the label, can be a grape variety or a wine region (VdT, IGT, DOC or DOCG).

We also know a bit more about the producer and vintage being included for the higher classified wines. We will now learn how the label on a bottle shows the full identity of the wine, and therefore contains additional details and illustrations designed for the consumer to understand the origin of the wine. *(Federdoc, 2022)*

The label provides a whole series of important information about the wine and its characteristics, growing conditions, age and location - and must be whole and verifiable. *(Federdoc, 2022)* In this regard, for a common link for all European wines, The European Community issued a series of precise labelling rules in order to legislate on a European level. The E.C. legislation brings together wines with DOC and DOCG labels under the one acronym DOP (PDO in Italian - 'Protected Designation of Origin') *(Federdoc, 2022)*

As well as these uniting classification systems, there are a few other unique terms seen on Italian wine labels that will help you to read and identify them.

Riserva:

This means wines aged longer than the standard requirement - which differs by denomination, but it's typically a year longer than required to be this classification.

Superiore:

Wines with higher quality grapes and a higher alcohol content.

Classico:

These are wines that come from historical wine regions and will often be included on the label - for example, our Day 1 example of 'Chianti Classico.'

(Vino Vest, 2021)

Fig 15. Reading a wine bottle label

The above illustration refers to the below labelling practises:

1. The Designation of Origin mention

It specifies the proper Designation of Origin type

2. Specific traditional mentions DOC or DOCG (PDO)

As mentioned above - DOC or DOCG may be accompanied (or replaced by) the acronym DOP which defines, at a European level, those wines with Designation of Origin.

3. Nominal volume of wine

The nominal volume of wine must be stated in litres, centilitres, or millilitres and advises content volume in the bottle

4. Vintage

Starting from the 2010 harvest, the indication of the year is mandatory for all Italian DOCG and DOC wine types (except for sparkling, fizzy, and fortified)

5. Name of the bottler

The company name of the corresponding bottler must always be specified. (For sparkling wines, the producer may replace it with the bottler company name, or the producer/retailer in these permitted cases, must appear together with the name of the municipality where the production plant is located and its home Member State (Italy).)

6. Indication of origin

The term "produced in" (or equivalent terms such as "wine of", "product of", etc.) followed by the name of the Member State - this shows where the grapes were harvested and vinified.

7. Indication of the batch

Numbering that indicates a set of bottles belonging to the same group. As a rule, it is usually preceded by the letter "L".

8. Sulphites

It indicates that the product has been treated with allergens such as sulphur dioxide.

This statement is mandatory when the sulphite content exceeds 10 mg/litre.

9. Alcohol strength

The alcohol content must be expressed in units or in half units of percentage by volume - for example 12% vol.12.5% vol. and may include the wording "actual alcoholic strength" or "actual alcohol" or just by the abbreviation "alc".

DAY 3 GLOSSARY OF TERMS

Agronomy - the science of soil management and crop production.

Vino bianco - white wine

Vino rosato - rosé wine

Vino rosso - red wine

Vinification - the conversion of grape juice or other vegetable extract into wine by fermentation

DAY 4

ITALY'S WINE TERROIRS: AN OVERVIEW

While we are delving into the implications of regions on the types of wines produced, and before getting to the grape types grown there in tomorrow's session, we come to the definition of 'terroirs' - and I promise this isn't a typo of 'terrier.'

A broad definition of the 'terroir' when referring to it in a wine context, is offered in its simplest form by Daniele Cernilli (aka 'Dr Wine' - **what** a title) who says "Terroir is about soil, weather, culture and tradition that makes the wine". *(The Buyer, 2018)*

For her, this implies it is about the winemaker producing the wine.

But for many winemakers the 'terroir' is in fact about the soil, microclimate, location and elevation of their vineyard - i.e some of which is in fact beyond their control.

What can be agreed therefore, is that the term expresses a concept of the wine being deeply connected to place (i.e the natural aspects of the terroir) as well as the people (i.e. process choices made by the vignaiolo). *(Uncorked in Italy, 2014)*

The pleasure in understanding Italian 'terroir' is knowing that when you pour a glass of wine that there is one of those beautiful heritage stories behind it; of its place and its people.

There is no exact proof or evidence as to how the natural aspects of a terroir, combined with the choices made by the vignaiolo, create tastes and aromas in the wine... but they are certainly there and they change by harvest, from year to year. *(Uncorked in Italy, 2014)*

The natural aspects of terroir, to do with location and climate, include the below conditions:

- The soil and soil type
- The lay of the land (flat, hills, mountains)
- Proximity to natural water sources, i.e the sea, lakes or rivers

- Exposition (which direction the vineyard faces)
- Height above sea level
- Impact of wind
- Climate (seasonal variation, temperatures and rainfall etc.)
- Exposure to sunlight
- Temperature changes between day and night

The aspect of terroir linked to choices of the vignaiolo / winemaker, include the below:

- Choice of grape variety and grape combinations
- The planting and growing methods
- Methods of pruning, fertilizing and looking after the vines
- The time of harvest
- Processes for turning grapes into into wine (including the type of container for fermentation; time left with the skins during fermentation; time on the lees after fermentation, temperature controls etc)
- The time, container and methods dedicated to ageing

(Uncorked in Italy, 2014)

The result is that many winemakers choose to combine these aspects into evidence that their wines are 'terroir-driven' - a phrase I will use because frankly what other phrase would cut it?

There is no doubt that consumers want to focus on unique native grapes, but also value the importance of its region, terroir-driven identity? (Oh God, it caught on sooner than I realised)

The winemakers are understandably just keen to show that their wine somehow expresses the best qualities that their land can impart to the wine. *(The Buyer, 2018)*

Some observers, such as Ian d'Agata - a highly respected author on Italian grapes and wine - lament the wealth of local grape varieties that no other country possesses, and which we will explore in huge detail in the following chapter. It is true that with almost 400 native grape varieties, surely it is the huge variety of resulting aromas and flavours that should be celebrated.

Indeed, authors such as d'Agata would argue this is where the future lies for Italian wineries, who need to harness the potential of Italy's diverse grapes. *(The buyer, 2018)* In d-Agata's most recent book 'Italy's Native Wine Grape Terroirs' he acknowledges that the reason for this delay in Italy adopting a similar approach to the Appellation system as, say, the French (who embraced the terroir idea centuries ago) is due to italy's only relatively recent Nationhood. Italy has only existed as a single country since Unification in 1861, and as such, d'Agata and some others believe that the understanding of terroir in Italy is therefore a far more recent development and still being formed. *(Italy's Native Wine Grape Terroirs, 2020)*

Looking at this idea further, a few Italian grapes are now almost as well known as the international varieties themselves due to this lack of a terroir understanding being commonplace - e.g. names that will become scarily familiar to you from tomorrow onwards if not already, like Sangiovese, Glera and Nebbiolo.

But it would be right to suggest that most consumers have never heard of the majority of others. They are not really household names, nor something which jumps out to the average consumer when choosing a bottle in a shop or restaurant – which poses a challenge for Italian wineries when exporting to the powerhouse buyers of the UK and USA for example, *(The Buyer, 2018)* as consumers lack any known regional identity or grape name in terms of familiarity with most Italian wines.

The more I have looked into the 'terroirs' and the evidence to whether a wine does truly display a sense of the place it comes from, the more difficult the research becomes and the deeper a dark hole of different opinions you delve into.

If we buy into the value of 'terroir-driven' impacts on wine (for the sake of this entire chapter please) then the argument in its favour is an evidence that wine will show how the land 'has its say' - i.e. the land and climate allow the "nature of the environment to express itself in the wine." *(The Buyer, 2018)*

That is in fact not as wafty and holistic as it may sound - as it refers to the above scientific aspects that can be proven after production.

What's more, if we are to take this approach then we also willingly appreciate that **how** this is applied by each winery (i.e. the winemakers' choices) can vary it significantly. For example, soil health and quality is certainly not down to nature alone, and adding chemicals or moving to organic farming for example, will all make significant differences in the approach to expressing a 'terroir'. *(The Buyer, 2018)*

Now that I have muddied the waters even further, for which you are most welcome, let's look at examples where whatever you want to call it, there is sound evidence of natural aspects having a dramatic effect on wine production.

To set the scene, each native grape variety has specific DNA that defines it and determines the chemical content of the wine. Over time, the grape variety becomes increasingly adapted to the conditions of its environment and the taste becomes even more representative of its terroir. (*Wine Alchemy, 2020*)

For example, the Nebbiolo grape from Valtellina in the Lombardy region, is recognisably the same grape, yet tastes completely differently to, the Nebbiolo grapes grown in Barolo or Barbaresco (Piemonte). It's even differentiable even further, according to each subzone or its vineyard.

Fig 16. Nebbiolo Taste profile

Sticking with the Nebbiolo example as the most extensively different grape dependent on its terroir, we must understand that because it has resisted most efforts to grow it successfully elsewhere, it became so linked to the Langhe, the area within southern Piemonte zones of Barolo and Barbaresco mentioned above.

To the North of the Langhe, however, and deep in the Alpine foothills, there are other substantial Nebbiolo areas such as Carema; then up as far as Valle d'Aosta, and; to the East, in Ghemme and Gattinara. *(New York Times, 2014)*

Though these wines in some ways reflect Barolo and Barbaresco, each is distinctive and reflects the climate, soils, terrain and all other factors listed above, and is not trying to imitate its namesake.

Nebbiolos from outside the Langhe subzone offer something different - and their personal terroirs are what makes them distinctive. They may not reach the heights of the best Barolos and Barbarescos in terms of wine aficionados' appreciation, but in a way that doesn't matter here, and we will look at such examples to be evaluated on their own terms.

Take a Carema of Luigi Ferrando for example, or a Valtellina from ArPePe and a Spanna from Vallana (pardon the rhyme) and you have yourself a completely different type of Nebbiolo *(New York Times, 2014)* just thanks to the terroir being outside of the Langhe and temperable to the expected.

So what does this really mean for a wine that varies by terroir? Well in this particular example, it means the Nebbiolo grapes tend to be grown in cooler climates at higher elevations than the Langhe, therefore it doesn't create the expected Barolos and Barbaresco texture.

The variations on Nebbiolo, like the above, tend to create wines that are lighter in colour; more delicate; less tannic and; more acidic. (*(New York Times, 2014)* The latter of these regarding tannin and acidity, mean that they simply will be accessible earlier than Barolos and Barbarescos, though they still require bottle ageing.

Historically, particularly in Valtellina and Carema (see map above) the greatest problem facing wine producers was ripening the grapes, since only those who farmed meticulously and limited their yields from the Northern edge area, were able to obtain consistency. (*(New York Times, 2014)* This is where the winemakers' impact comes into play, and a bit of pot luck on your positioning I guess you could argue.

Over the last two decades, viticulture in these bordering Nebbiolo regions has greatly improved and moved with the times, while climate change has taken its toll on raised temperature changes as well. Nowadays, you will rarely find wines that seem under ripe due to increasingly warmer climates in those regions that were previously cooler.

If you want my pick, for a Nebbiolo from outside the Langhe and something accessible and reliably delightful, then the Produttori di Carema, available from the Co-Op (UK) and alike for US$23 or so, is the one to go for. ArPePes also never fail and you can try the simple version or more expensive cuvées if looking to spend a bit more.

Looking at the other most well-known grapes and their diversity according to terroir, the famed Italian Sangiovese from Tuscany, (get ready again to cover in huge detail tomorrow) is produced in many ways including the Chianti Classico we tried on Day 1. It perfectly reflects the Tuscan landscape and culture the grapes were grown in; and match local cuisine specialties like bistecca alla Fiorentina or wild boar. *(Vino Travels italy, 2015)*

As you now know from trying it, Chianti Classico is rightfully one of the most popular wines throughout the world. There are many clones of it that you can find throughout Tuscany, dependent on the region and even the sub-region the grapes are conditioned by.

Tuscany alone has a number of different expressions of this Sangiovese grape according to terroir, so let's look even further into the breadth of its diversity even just within the region of Tuscany:

Chianti Classico

Classically considered to be the best quality, the historical and renowned area of the Chianti Classic DOCG even has its own subzones:

- Gaiole in Chianti
- Greve in Chianti
- Radda in Chianti
- Castellina in Chianti
- Panzano in Chianti
- Castelnuovo Berardegna
- Barberino Val d'Elsa

(Vino Travels italy, 2015)

So as a reminder of Day 2's wisdom, Chianti Classico DOCG requires at least 85% Sangiovese grapes, and is permitted to have additional indigenous grapes blended for the remaining 15% - these can include Canaiolo, Colorino, Mammolo for example. *(Vino Travels, 2015)*

However, outside of the classic area of Chianti, Tuscany, there are also **three** other areas that are recognized for producing some of Italy's top wines from the same Sangiovese grape, including Brunello di Montalcino, Vino Nobile di Montepulciano and Morellino di Scansano. *(Vino Travels italy, 2015)*

- Brunello di Montalcino

Brunello di Montalcino DOCG is produced 100% by the Sangiovese grape clone known as 'Sangiovese Grosso,' and is produced in the town of Montalcino in a warmer South - Western section of Tuscany that produces riper, fuller bodied versions of Sangiovese due to the terroir-driven (stop it) natural climate impacts, as well as winemakers ageing it for four years in barriques and 5 years for a Riserva.

- Vino Nobile di Montepulciano

About 30 minutes East of Montalcino is the town of Montepulciano where Vino Nobile di Montepulciano DOCG is produced. *(Vino Travels italy, 2015)* Now I am sorry to do this to you but this is not to be confused with the grape itself Montepulciano, which we will be trying in its Abruzzo form together this evening.

This type of Sangiovese clone is called 'Prugnolo Gentile', which is required to produce at a minimum of 70% of Sangiovese grape, with additional grapes permitted again.

This terroir is sandier and it has less fluctuations in temperature, but still produces wines that are fuller than the original Chianti versions.

- Morellino di Scansano

Lastly, if you're keeping up with the clones of Sangiovese grape based on terroir, we visit the final area of Tuscany that also uses a clone variety; Scansano - which is widely considered the 'New Tuscany,' located in the Maremma area in the South of the region, and we will look at more closely later in the book when studying new trends and areas.

(Vino Travels, 2015)

This exciting wine, Morellino di Scansano DOCG in particular, is using the 'Morellino' Sangiovese clone, a darker version of the grape and here is produced with at least 85% of Morellino. Maremma contains both volcanic soils that add minerality to the wine and some sea fossils - since this area was once a marshland that was drained in the 1930s.

The Morellino clone of Sangiovese grapes in this subzone specifically, result in fresh, rounder grapes with some chewiness and impacting the wine produced. *(Vino Travels, 2015)*

Fig 17. Sangiovese Taste Profile

This is just the beginning when it comes to Sangiovese, but this covers Tuscany and the versions of the same grape cloned according to its terroir and hopefully a relatively digestible example of today's topic.

Our Tuscan journey doesn't stop here, and I look forward to taking you through the wider story of other grapes grown here and the diversity of wines in this most famous of regions.

Leaving Central Italy for now, and travelling West to the island of Sardinia where there is a lot of shellfish, it is perfectly logical that one of the local grapes, Vermentino, would flourish in this area with its minerality and citrus. *(Vino Travels Italy, 2015)*

Vermentino di Sardegna, from Sardinia, (the second biggest of all the Mediterranean islands) has a diversity of varying landscapes almost rivalling that of a whole country.

Modern day Sardinian Vermentino examples now rank alongside Vermentino di Gallura DOCG from the North-East in quality and expressiveness. *(Wine Alchemy, 2018)*

While Vermentino has long grown on the island, increasing popularity means that it's now found all over the island and stretches beyond the original terroirs.

This reflects the attention to quality that gained momentum in the 1980s and 1990s in the new age of Italian wine - during this time, the Sardinian vineyards were replanted with better clones and training, while wineries modernised and new ventures were established. *(Wine Alchemy, 2018)*

Fig 18. Island of Sardinia

Looking at such a large island, you can see how it would have many different terroirs, which means diversity in the grapes. For example, the natural assets at play here range from coastal to inland locations, sea level to altitudes, and on flat land or mountainside terrains. *(Wine Alchemy, 2018)*

This means the terroir soils vary too, from limestone to dusty sand and clay. In neighbouring Gallura the granite and wind has a distinct implication on the resulting wine from the same Vermentino grapes.

An area I have been to and so can speak from experience, is Cagliari in the South of the island - Here, Paùli's at Cantine Sociale di Monserrato winery is the oldest cooperative in Sardinia, dating from 1924 and where Vermentino grapes make up about 35% of production.

They produce both the Ghineo from 2017, an entry-level wine with saline kick and at a very affordable £5.00 (US $6), as well as an Evento Oro, their top cuvée and very fruity also at a great price of £8.00 (US$10).

Meanwhile, at the Santadi winery started in 1960 in Sulcis, the Vermentino vines grow on sand and clay and the terroir is dry. Here, under the guidance of the well-known oenologist Giacomo Tachis, the quality of the wines hit new peaks, but they remain very good value. The below for example from this sub-zone are excellent examples of very different expressions to that which I tried in Cagliari:

- The Villa Solais 2017; this is a blend of 85% Vermentino and 15% Nuragus, an indigenous white grape, and still leaves the Vermentino signature acidity and salinity. (Priced at £13, US$16)

- Cala Silente 2017; this is a Classic Vermentino; its aromas (everyone get their Aroma Wheels out) are herbs on the nose, as well as apple, peach and pineapple. (Priced at £12, US$15) *(Wine Alchemy, 2018)*

So, in wrapping up on Vermentinos, the Vermentino di Sardegna may once have been inferior to Gallura, but this is no longer the case - and they are now appreciated as two different expressions of the best of their terroirs. *(Wine Alchemy, 2018)*

And Vermentino di Sardegna isn't just a holiday wine, and can be found at home in our supermarkets and bars, so buy it with confidence and enjoy.

As we look finally to terroirs in Southern Italy, Puglia is Italy's second largest wine producing region and has a formidable array of natural assets to help encourage prolific wine making - the warm Mediterranean climate, sunshine and light breeze make for a near-perfect environment for viticulture, (*Wine Searcher, 2020*) rivalled by those toughing it in harsher terrains. The region's geology is heavy with limestone and iron-rich deposits, most visible in the soils around the Colline Joniche Tarantine hills and the Itria Valley. (*Wine Searcher, 2020*)

Fig 19. Region of Puglia

In fact Puglia is seizing an opportunity in the modern wine world to present concentrated reds to rival the best from even Australia and South America, which we will explore below, and says a lot about the transformational ability of regions as grape-growing, and then reputations, evolve.

The region's richly fertile soils and beautiful climate make it perfect for growing grapes. It has a relatively hot and dry climate that's tempered by cool breezes from the surrounding water, resulting in expressive clones of delicious wines. *(Especially Puglia, 2018)*

The incredibly diverse geography of just this one region produces wines that are endlessly varied in terroir. Puglia currently has 29 DOC and 4 DOCG wine subzones, mostly concentrated in the Salento region at the very heel *(Especially Puglia, 2018)* which is near 'Lecce' marked on the above map.

If you love your Italian wines, which hopefully you will by the end of this book - this is definitely the region to celebrate in all its cork-popping glory. The below are the major grapes you will come across when you first dive into the beautiful world of Pugliese wine, and the terroirs that shape how they differ by area:

- **Primitivo**

The Primitivo grape is the same as the California Zinfandel, which you are likely to know and have tried - and is also one of the main grape families in Italy which we have not explored in enough detail until now.

It is predominantly grown in the Puglia region on the South Coast, but also in Veneto and a few other select areas of Italy.

In the past, it was also used as a blending grape in Tuscany and Piemonte. *(Vino Vest, 2022)* The name in its Italian context originates from old Italian meaning "early ripening" which is true to its early Puglian harvest in August. *(Especially Puglia, 2018)* The grape in general is sensitive to drought, high temperatures and frost, and the result is a wine with a naturally high sugar and alcohol content. *(Especially Puglia, 2018)*

Fig 20. Area of Primitivo in Puglia

The four major appellations of the Primitivo grape in Italy today are as follows:

- Primitivo di Manduria DOC
- Primitivo di Manduria Dolce Naturale DOCG
- Gioia del Colle Primitivo DOC
- Salento IGT.

However, the early ripening Primitivo vine produces low to medium yields depending on the grower, the methods and the terroir. If, for example, there is an uncharacteristic temperature or seasonal fluctuations or spring frost, then this will dramatically impact the harvest that year on any of the above expressions. *(Especially Puglia, 2018)*

In general it is fair to say that the Primitivo vines in Manduria (see map above) grow on iron-rich clay soils mixed with large rocks, and will also thrive on sandy soils; black soils from alluvial deposits and even; volcanic and calcareous soils. *(Especially Puglia, 2018)*

Conventionally, the Primitivo vine is alberello trained but recently some vineyards have adopted trellis systems in more recent times. It is also a grape that will suffer from its terroir when it over-ripens quickly making it vulnerable to moulds and humidity. In these instances we see the negative effect of a changeable terroir and how this impacts a harvest - but importantly shows us the argument for this being an essential consideration and classification of the wine.

Fig 21. Illustration of Italian Grapes in vine

In wrapping up a boggling Day 4 on the admittedly complicated, but necessary, topic of terroirs, we end with a sense of (hopefully) united agreement that the classification of wine quality by a focus on terroir is where Italian wine should, and will, be heading. Not only to make up for the refined wine history of the French approach, but because it is a necessary further identification method in a sea of outstanding Italian wines - the same reason the DOCG was invented for example all those years ago.

In recent years there have been all manner of projects identifying the best sites for this exploration and for evidence to support the argument further. They are from the likes of Soave, Lessini, Chianti Classico, Barolo, Prosecco, Brunello, and Montefalco Sagrantino which I will leave you to delve further into on your own time if your appetite for more detail gets the better of you.

Furthermore, the terroir-driven profiles of increasingly popular Italian whites are leading the way, especially in Alto Adige DOC and the Lugana DOC areas, as wine lovers learn to appreciate their clean profiles. *(Daily Seven-Fifty, 2020)* Being able to draw from Italy's North-Eastern natural resources; the Dolomite mountains and Lake Garda respectively; these wines emulate their respective terroirs in the glass, with their memorable aromas, acidity and fruity flavours straight from their orchards. *(Daily Seven-Fifty, 2020)*

SUMMARY OF DAY 4

In summary, we have covered today what it means for a wine to be 'terroir - driven' and whether this has a place in a modern-day appreciation and explanation of wines.

I have outlined the definitions of terroirs in this context, and how it encapsulates the natural aspects of location and climate, as well as the choices of a vignaiolo / winemaker in their varied methods and processes.

Next we looked at some of the main grapes that have a family of clones which vary according to their terroir - either from within the same region or beyond - and the implications of those different terroirs on the grapes and resulting wines.

Firstly the Nebbiolo grape which diversifies hugely depending on its terroir, and is commonly linked to the Langhe. But looking in more detail today we discovered that North of the Langhe and deep in the Alpine foothills, there are other substantial Nebbiolo-growing areas and some excellent wines arising from there.

Then, onto the Sangiovese grape we covered the famous Chianti Classico and the many expressions of it that you can find throughout Tuscany, depending on the region and even the sub-region.

Next we went West to Sardinia, where the Vermentino has long grown on certain parts of the island, but with increasing popularity it is now found all over and stretches far beyond the original terroirs.

And finally, to the tip of the South where we ended with the wonderful world of Pugliese wine, and the terroirs that shape it by area: Primitivo in particular, which we learned is genetically identical to the American Zinfandel, has come a long way from being used in inexpensive red wine blends, to being the star grape of some exceptional varietals we celebrate today from several terroirs.

So, we have ended today hopefully with an understanding of wines according to their terroir, and covered the movement towards where Italian wine should, and is likely, to be heading with this approach. In recent years there have been all manner of projects identifying the best sites and expressions of grape by terroir, and the examples we have looked at today suggest that it is with good reason we consider these assets when drinking and matching Italy's finest wines.

DAY 4 WINE

Our Day 4 wine to celebrate and enjoy together, is a Montepulciano d'Abruzzo - from the Abruzzo region we covered yesterday and in some of its terroirs today - and not to be confused with yesterday's Montalcino (it just sounds confusingly similar but has no link)

As we will cover in more detail tomorrow when looking at grape families, the stand-out grape of Abruzzo is the native red Montepulciano; a poster-child in this central Italian area.

There is one DOCG example of today's tipple from the region, called Montepulciano d'Abruzzo Colline Teramane DOCG. But what we are going to try is an affordable and accessible version of this, of which there are many. Montepulciano d'Abruzzo Terre dei Vestini DOC; from the Terre dei Vestini terroir, an area which includes the lands on the Adriatic coast and the inland hills of the Pescara province - my recent holiday destination should anyone be interested.

The Terre dei Vestini subzone attempted to tame Abruzzo's Montepulciano grape, by trying to infuse it with more elegance and style. Producers have been very successful in doing so, by refining the ageing process and therefore softening the slightly harsh characteristics.

Our Montepulciano d'Abruzzo Terre dei Vestini DOC you will see from the label and name is a DOC wine, therefore made from Montepulciano grapes at 90-100% with the permission to add local varieties between 0-10% only. *(Italian Wine Guide, 2022)* The grapes are cultivated entirely or partially in 20 municipalities in the Pescara province. *(Italian Wine Guide, 2022)*

You will see on pouring a glass that this wine is an intense ruby red shade wine with shades of violet - the aroma is intense, with a hint of harvested red fruits, dried herbs and even some spices. It is a very affordable £16 (US$20) and you're welcome for bringing this back to wine prices we don't have to remortgage houses for - it is a brilliant wine to get hold of easily and serve with pork, wine, beef / veal and stews. Basically for your delightful average (non-vegetarian) dinner party this wine is going to hit the mark.

It is fairly strong - the minimum alcohol concentration of this variety is 12,5%, and it has a mandatory ageing period of 18 months, of which 9 should be in a barrels and 3 months in the bottle *(Italian Wine Guide, 2022)* - and it has a further storage potential of up to 5 years if anyone could ever possibly leave a bottle of this unopened for that long. *(Italian Wine Guide, 2022)* If this same wine is aged for a minimum of 24 months, 9 of which in barrels and 6 months in bottle, it gets the distinction of Terre dei Vestini **Riserva** DOC as previously explained.

Today, there are many quality producers of a similar Montepulciano d'Abruzzo wine in the region, and the best wines exhibit the grape's naturally high acidity, tannin and alcohol rather than just a high classification status. Montepulciano d'Abruzzo wines can represent excellent value for money, as is the case with this one, and it is widely exported for our drinking pleasure from home.

Other examples, and with slightly varying price points for different occasions include the below:

- Masciarelli Marina Cvetic Riserva 2016; a world-class Montepulciano d'Abruzzo with grapes from eight vineyard sites across the Abruzzo region and priced approx. £18
- Cantina Zaccagnini; a great value red wine produced in the Pescara province. Each bottle has a small piece of dried grape vine tied around its neck that makes the brand memorable and I loved seeing when in Pescara. Priced approx. £12.
- Pasetti Harimann; a medium-bodied wine with well-balanced tannin

(Vino Vest, 2022) Priced up to £30

DAY 4 TAKE AWAY LESSON

How to smell wine professionally?

Since we are now armed with an Aroma Wheel, and have spent the last few days looking at terroirs and regions as well as the types of wines produced there, I think we are ready to get our honkers into our glasses and identify basic aromas. We don't need to be experts yet, and this could be a great exercise to try again at the end of Day 7 and see just how far you have come. But for now, I have done diagrams for red and white wines below that will set the scene for the main flavours you expect to find 'mid-nose-in-glass.' Wine's flavours come from aroma compounds that are released during fermentation. *(Wine Folly, 2020)* So in the action of smelling a wine, the alcohol evaporates into the air and carries aroma compounds into your nose.

Each wine can contain hundreds of different aroma compounds and each compound can further affect the flavour of a wine. And even more diversely, our brains often have multiple responses to one aroma, which means not only might one person 'like' a smell that another doesn't, it may be that you also genuinely smell roses as a common example, when detecting lychee fruit in some wine varieties. *(Wine Folly, 2020)*

But confidence is king here, like with many things in life - so get that nose stuck in and follow the below steps to identify key aromas and sniff like a wine boss:

- **Transfer your wine from a bottle with an aerator (ideally) or into a decanter.** (Tip: You can let your wine decant for anywhere from one hour to three hours)
- **After that time, transfer the wine again from the decanter to a glass.** (Tip: Make sure to pour at an angle to maximise the amount of oxygen exposure)
- **Brush up on how to hold a wine glass from Day 1's lesson, for the best experience**
- **Raise your glass and smell the air inside the bowl of your glass**
- **Experiment with different smelling techniques and sniffs** (I'm being serious - try smelling with a long, deep inhalation as well as little, shorter strong sniffs. There's no right or wrong way to use your own nose folks)
- **Consider what the wine aromas make you think of - and be creative here.** (Tip: There are hundreds of chemical compounds and subtleties in a single glass of wine.. get creative

with what comes to mind and don't be shy, it's unlikely to be wrong)

- **And finally; Look for the most obvious - the fruit flavours** (diagram above to help)

Wine smelling is an excellent skill to add to your ever-growing connoisseur repertoire - it helps you select the right wine in the first place, and is a conduct performed as we grow in wine expertise, before finally being able to share aromas with friends and family over the dinner table.

DAY 4 GLOSSARY OF TERMS

vignaiolo - winemaker

aficionado - a person who is very knowledgeable and enthusiastic about an activity, subject, or pastime - i.e. "aficionados of the finest wines"

alberello trained - to grow like single trees

DAY 5

NATIVE GRAPES BY REGION

Fig 22. Italian grapes by region

ITALY'S GRAPE VARIETIES

Italy's vineyards are home to more than 2,000 grape varieties, *(Wine Searcher, 2020)* The most-sustained and best-known Italian grapes, which by now I hope are even slightly familiar, are Sangiovese, Barbera, Nebbiolo, Montepulciano and Pinot Grigio; *(Wine Searcher, 2020)* although technically the latter is more French than Italian and you can sound even more widely European wine-savvy by knowing that.

These varieties cover thousands of acres of vineyards, right across Italy and can mostly all be found in multiple regions. In contrast, the country is also home to very rare, and in some cases threatened, little-known grapes such as Centesimino and Dorona, *(Wine Searcher, 2020)* which are found only in very small numbers and in just one or two specific regions.

In this section, we are going to cover both of these varying types of grape families as well as everything in between, to give you an understanding of the scope and growing patterns of varietals in the different regions and why.

Let's look at some of the bigger flagship regions of Italian wine to get us started on the grape trail - hoping that some of Day 3 and 4 went in one ear and stayed there, as it's not all straightforward. The wine names are what are likely to stick for the sake of choosing and honouring great wines, but it is important to know the grapes and identification of grapes' areas to be able to use this knowledge fully.

Out of the more than 350 grape varieties acknowledged by the Italian Ministry of Agriculture and Forestry, the major grapes to note are:

Red Wine Grapes:

- Nebbiolo
- Aglianico
- Sangiovese
- Barbera
- Corvina
- Dolcetto
- Montepulciano
- Negroamaro
- Nero d'Avola
- Primitivo
- Sagrantino

White Wine Grapes:

- Trebbiano
- Moscato Blanc
- Malvasia Bianca
- Vermentino
- Pinot Grigio
- Greco
- Arneis
- Cataratto
- Pigato

(Briscoe Bites, 2022)

NORTHERN ITALY

When we look at Northern Italy, it is the area closest to the foothills of the Alps as well as the plains of the River Po - which tends to mean a moderate climate with dry, short summers.

The Alps run the length of the Northern Italian border and therefore shield the area from rain.

Like the River Po, other bodies of water that provide climatic moderation to the more inland areas include lakes in other areas of Italy such as Lake Garda. *(Briscoe Bites, 2022)*

The climate and the lie of the land impact everything from the types of grapes grown, to when and how they can be harvested - and in the case of Northern Italy the above bears a significant impact on production.

So let's break down a few different regions' native grapes within Northern Italy…

Trentino Alto Adige

Trentino Alto Adige is Italy's most Northern wine region, with a moderate climate and short, dry summers with low rainfall during the growing season - I can only wish we could say the same for the UK.

Because most vineyards are planted at altitude, they experience daytime growing (or a 'diurnal range' - steady) which produces aromatic white wines, such as the well-loved Pinot Grigio. Here, Pinot Grigio is produced in a dry style and fruit flavours of citrus and apples.

Just south of Alto Adige is Trentino - an area of grapes planted at high altitude and similar to those found in Alto Adige, but those planted along the valley floor will be notably different, with a lower level of acidity and riper aromas. Moving swiftly further down the country, we come to the iconic Veneto region.

Veneto

Giving more time to Veneto in the North of Italy, the celebrated and one of the largest wine regions in Italy, celebrates a huge selection of grapes and appellations.

The best-known is Prosecco, a sparkling wine made from the Glera grape; Glera is undoubtedly one of Italy's most famous grape varieties, without most people being aware of it. Known the world over as Prosecco, the Glera grape again is the golden star behind the name; exclusive to Italy and is the main ingredient for Italy's most celebrated sparkling tipple. It's a green-skinned grape variety that thrives in the cool conditions in the North-East, particularly across the regions of Veneto and leading into Friuli. *(Virgin Wines, 2022)*

Interestingly, Prosecco is Italy's largest DOC and the classification as such keeps production within the region. Production wise, Prosecco uses the tank method where secondary fermentation takes place in the tank rather than the bottle. From this infusion comes the full flavour of the original base wine in the resulting bottle of sparkling.

For Prosecco, this method means that for a fraction of the price, there are some great mimicking wines available that emulate their expensive counterparts, but of course you can never beat the original. We will look at the best Proseccos later when delving into sparkling wines in all their glory on Day 6.

The region also produces Soave, a white wine made from the Garganega grape, and Valpolicella; a red wine made from a blend based on Corvina grapes and varying in style from light, racy wines to very full-bodied Amarone wines. *(Vinate Roots, 2016)*

Staging with whites for now, Soave is Garganega. Again, one can never be too explanatory in the case of Italian wine as it is not an easy business - Soave is the name to associate with 'Garganega' - the grape. It is of medium body, medium acidity and medium-level of fruit maturity when it comes to flavours, such as stone fruits. *(Briscoe Bites, 2022)*

In Italy, boundaries of certain appellations have expanded, hence the difficulty in banding grape families entirely to certain regions, so the term 'Classico' is used to differentiate wines produced from grapes sourced from the original wine region. *(Biscoe Bites, 2022)*

Soave, for example while we're on this grape, has two distinct sections to its production; the foothills to the North and the flat plains to the South of Veneto, near the river Po. The area of foothills to the North of the region are considered the 'Soave Classico.' Here, we find limestone and clay soils, along with some volcanic rock, where the cool growing soils and altitude of the vineyards, ensure a moderate climate that slows the ripening. *(Briscoe Bites, 2022)*

Other major grape varieties of the region are Corvina; (making Valpolicella - a red wine grape similar to Soave in that it contains the foothills elements above and is a thin-skinned variety with lowish tannins and high acidity) Garganega and; Rondinella *(Vino Vest, 2020)* but leaving Veneto for now, we move to the famous Piedmont.

Piemonte

It is hard not to cover this region in detail for both the wines produced there and the grape families within it, as both are so prolific and so central to the story of Italian winemaking.

So, in addition to other grape varieties you can see from the table above that are present in this region (Barbaresco, Barbera, Moscato, Arneis and Roero) we are going to look at the Barolo DOCG. Barolo DOCG is a hilly region, with vineyard slopes reaching 300 to 500 metres high.

While the altitude cools down the temperature, it also allows the grape to receive consistent sunlight throughout the day; both helping to extend the grapes' growing season. *True* Barolo DOCG must be made from 100% Nebbiolo grape. *(Briscoe Bites, 2022)*

This is worth a side note here, in the interest of us all learning a complicated system and not wanting to make it even harder - *When you say Barolo, you must hear Nebbiolo! Nebbiolo is a red wine grape that has a high level of acid and tannin, but is very light in colour. It is a slow grape and a late ripener - once a winemaker from Barolo said on a podcast that Nebbiolo is the "first to flower but the last to fully ripen" *(Briscoe Bites, 2022)* and this is a helpful description to keep in mind.

So what happens when a Barolo is able to "fully" ripen I hear you ask? It develops stronger, perfumed aromas that you will see from all heavily ripened grape varieties - similar to roses for example - but the WSET officially describes the aromas released as sour cherries, herbs and dried flowers. *(Briscoe Bites, 2022)*

These wines are typically full-bodied; very high in acidity and tannins (and are certainly intended for ageing. Barolo for example is required to age for three years prior to release; 18 months of which must be in oak, hence the heavy influence of oak barrels on its release. *(Briscoe Bites, 2022)*

Tuscany and Central Italy

The Tuscany wine region is one of the most prolific in all of Europe, and we are now familiar with some of the internationally-recognised wines of all styles, found here. Sangiovese grapes flourish in Tuscany, under a number of different names (depending on the sub-region), *(Vintage Roots, 2016)* and it is used in the production of a range of Italian wines – including Chianti.

In terms of native vines, Sangiovese are the most widespread and are the main base of many of the best of the region's red wines such as those we visited above - besides just Chianti Classico; also the Vino Nobile di

Montepulciano, Brunello di Montalcino and Carmignano *(Wine Searcher, 2019)*

Other indigenous varieties widely spread among Tuscan wines are Canaiolo Nero, Colorino, Ciliegiolo and Aleatico for reds; and Vermentino, Malvasia del Chianti and Trebbiano Toscano for whites. *(Wine Searcher, 2019)*

In addition, on the Tyrrhenian coast, and in particular in the Maremma and on the island of Elba, Ansonica (or Inzolia) grapes are widespread, from which are produced white Tuscan wines of great interest and we will look at more closely as an emerging grape trend.

Widespread international varieties among Tuscan wines are Cabernet Sauvignon, Cabernet Franc and Merlot; particularly true of the Bolgheri area and often used as complementary vines to the Sangiovese, as in the example of Chianti Classico and Carmignano. *(Vintage Roots, 2016)* Other international grape varieties from which Tuscan wines are produced are Syrah, in particular in Cortona and Lucchese; and Pinot Nero, in Casentino and Mugello.

As for Tuscan white wines, the most widely used international white grape varieties are Chardonnay; as with Pomino Bianco on the Florentine hills or in the

Maremma and ;Sauvignon Blanc, which is widespread on the Tyrrhenian coast in the region.

There is a reason the region is visited by holidaymakers the world over, and as well as its produce, the experience itself of visiting Tuscany is like no other. With endless wines to try, a large quantity of it is rightfully recognised as DOC and DOCG standards and holds its place in the global list of best wine regions.

Two of our personal favourite wines from Tuscany are:

- 'When We Dance' Chianti, a high-class Chianti made with Sangiovese, Colorino, and Canaiolo grapes
- DOCG Chianti Tenuta San Vito; an organic dark red wine with hints of cherry

Leaving Tuscany now, we look at a uniting grape variety in Central Italy - Trebbiano. There are at least six varieties of Trebbiano native to Italy, but Trebbiano Toscano, widely planted in Central Italy and globally in more recent times, is by far the most common. It is a white grape that produces crisp, light white wines.

The most common of the Trebbiano group is Trebbiano Toscano, and its family members, that spread to Marche and Abruzzo. The Trebbiano Toscano version we see here is a high cropper, with heavy weight and good fertility. *(Wine Searcher, 2022)* It is late-budding and needs lots of sun to ripen fully, which you find in abundance 'Under the Tuscan Sun' (sorry, couldn't help a book pun!) The best way to identify the specific Trebbiano Toscano in the vineyard is that the tips of its clusters are often split in two. While the variety is still to be associated with any outstanding dry white wines, there has been considerable research in recent years into optimising fruit quality in the vineyards of Tuscany.

Marche and Abruzzo

Still in Central Italy, in this instance we are looking at these two neighbouring regions in the same spotlight while analysing their grape trends (see layout of both regions in following chapter) Geographically, they run along the centre of Italy, and are both famous for their production of the wines explored together on Day 3; namely white Verdicchio and red Montepulciano grapes, respectively. But with more than 25,000 hectares of vineyards growing Trebbiano and Verdicchio grapes, I plan to first look at how Marche is famous for its high-acidity, green-hued white wines and age-worthy sweeter wines. *(Vintage Roots, 2016)*

Looking at the Trebbiano grape family in more detail and the differences with Tuscany and beyond, there are many distinct varieties with distant or unproven relationships to other grapes in the same group. *(Wine Searcher, 2022)* They do share some traits however; the most basic one (and I really am starting basic here) is that they are all white wine varieties.

In appearance, the bunches tend to be long and with large grapes; the berries are usually quite late ripening and; the vines are tough and adaptable to a range of terroirs. *(Wine Searcher, 2022)* Here you won't find the characteristic of the Tuscan Trebbiano of the tips of its clusters being split in two.

Fig 23. White wine Trebbiano Grape

Directly to the South of Marche, Abruzzo has over double the production area with

89,000 hectares of planted land, growing native grape varieties which also include Trebbiano. And confusingly, Trebbiano Toscano is one of the Trebbiano family also grown in Abruzzo. Many other Trebbiano d'Abbruzzo wines are thought to be made with the Bombino Bianco variety, reflected in the DOC regulations which require a minimum 85 percent component of any of the trio. *(Wine Searcher, 2022)*

Even the true Abruzzese Trebbiano have several forms - although the vines can typically be identified here by their large, five-lobed leaves which provide shade for the fruit and retain acidity. *(Wine Searcher, 2022)* The variety found here rarely gains the gold or reddish colours associated with other Trebbianos across Italy, and is an interesting example of appearance differing between the same grape family but in different regions. The two main variants vary in skin thickness and they tend to grow in double or treble clusters. *(Wine Searcher, 2022)*

While in Abruzzo, other grape varieties to acknowledge are Pecorino and Cocciola, as well as Chardonnay and Merlot which grows in several other areas. But Montepulciano d'Abruzzo, as explored on Day 3, is the most famous of the Abruzzo produce - and whose grapes we will look at more closely.

The most famous wines from this variety specifically come from the Abruzzo region, produced under the DOC title in vast volumes on the low hills around the Adriatic coast. *(Wine Searcher, 2021)*

Abruzzo's finest examples of Montepulciano come from the North of the region, in the Colline Teramane foothills. *(Wine Searcher, 2021)* Although slightly more expensive because of their DOCG status, these nonetheless represent excellent value for money for a wine of this standard and I highly recommend trying.

Two other notable Central Italian wines made from Montepulciano grapes nearby, are Rosso Conero and Rosso Piceno, both from the neighbouring Marche region. These wines are often of slightly higher quality officially, than their d'Abruzzo counterparts, they are in fact less well-known and celebrated; perhaps since their names share nothing about the grape variety from which they are produced. (Cue, takeaway lesson on Day 3 about the importance of wine labels and how to read them)

Another favourite of this quality wine type from the region I would recommend is:

- Jasci DOC Montepulciano d'Abruzzo, a deep red wine of dark fruits, vanilla and cinnamon.

Southern Italy

Historically, as the Greeks realised the trading potential of wine, the non-native varieties were brought first to Campania, Puglia, Basilicata and Calabria in the South. Its sunny climate became one of the largest grape biodiversity hotspots in the world.

The names of grapes, i.e. variations on the name greco or "Greek," reveal their origins as do the growing methods. In the South this is particularly interesting and impacts the wines grown here. In Puglia and Molise for example, methods remain as used by the ancient Romans.

In Campania, grape vines are draped onto tree trunks in a method also used throughout the centuries. In other regions though, vine stocks are tied into giant knots as a way of reducing yields with dramatic effects on the wines and flavours. So let's delve into the heel of Italy to look more closely at the grape families and trends…

Sicily

Moving to Sicily, the grape Nero d'Avola is the most important red wine variety found in the South of the region. It produces a fruity wine that is perfect for barrel-aging or blending it with other wines. (*Masterclass, 2021*)

But Sicily got our love when looking at wine varieties on Day 3, so moving on to regions of Northern Italy to celebrate some new grape families...

Campania

Campania is one of Italy's oldest wine regions and produces a range of red and white wines. The major grapes used are Aglianico, Greco, and Falanghina.

Looking at Aglianico more closely as the most common grape variety in this region, it is is a dark, musty varietal, introduced to Italy by the Greeks well over a thousand years ago, (*Masterclass, 2021*) and it continues to dominate the wine production in Campania, as well as Basilicata, even today. Its best-known expression is in Taurasi and aged Taurasi Riserva (we learned what this meant yesterday - phew) from Campania, and included in our 'Best of..' list below.

Fig 24. Campania Region

Top Campania Wines we recommend are: (*Vino Vest 2021*)

1. 2005 Mastroberardino Villa Dei Misteri Rosso Pompeiano IGT (Price: $211)

2. 2011 Quintodecimo 'Vigna Quintodecimo' Riserva, Taurasi DOCG (Price: $210)

Puglia

As visited briefly on Day 3, the "real" Puglia, at the heart of Southern Italy in its heel, is to be found in the South - even below the Brindisi–Taranto line. Here, the wines are made from grape varieties almost unique to the area.

The most obviously full-blooded Puglian grapes are Negroamaro and Primitivo, while Verdeca is the only salient example among the whites in this warm and otherwise red-dominated region. *(Wine Searcher, 2020)*

Primitivo grapes are at home in Manduria and Gioia del Colle, producing very robust wines known locally as "mirr test" ('hard wine' - seemingly more crass but very clear).

Negroamaro grape is more widespread in the region of Puglia and defines the red wines of the majority of southern Puglia's DOCs - namely Alezio, Matino, Galatina, Copertino, Nardo, Salice Salentino and Brindisi among a few others. *(Wine Searcher, 2020)*

The coastal town of Ostuni marks the Northern boundary of this grape zone, with its white wines based on the grape type Impigno (a crossing of Bombino Bianco and Quagliano) and outstanding rosés made from Ottavianello grapes (Cinsaut.)

In the middle of Puglia is a cluster of DOCs around the Barletta, where the Uva di Troia grape variety reigns supreme. *(Wine Searcher, 2020)* This low-yielding red variety is named after the nearby town of that name and is only now being recognized for its potential to make quality wines. This shift marks the new direction of some of the newer grape varieties in Italy being celebrated for their low-yield and high quality.

Sweet white wine, Moscato di Trani and Gravina - made from the Greco Bianco grapes, is a DOC classified wine found in the areas around those listed above. *(Wine Searcher, 2020)*

Sardinia

The portfolio of grape varieties planted on the South Western island of Sardinia, are different to those in any other Italian wine region and very distinctive.

The closest mainland wine regions to Sardinia are Tuscany and Lazio, and yet the key varieties used in these two regions of the commonly found Central Italian grapes Sangiovese, Montepulciano, Barbera and Trebbiano, are almost nowhere to be seen in Sardinia's vineyards. *(Wine Searcher, 2020)*

Instead, Sardinia offers European grape varieties of French and Spanish origin, exemplified by Grenache - but called Cannonau on the island.

You will also find the grape groups Carignan, plus its distinct clonal variants; Bovale di Spagna and Bovale Grande, as well as Cabernet Sauvignon. *(Wine Searcher, 2020)*

The 'most native' grape varieties to find here are Malvasia and Vermentino, and perhaps as an island off the mainland it should be expected that different influences are present, and certainly make the wine production interesting.

Of these two, Vermentino is more widely planted on the island of Corsica and Southern France, so wouldn't necessarily be thought of as Italian anyway (often under the name Rolle we saw earlier). Muscat Blanc (or Moscato Bianco), synonymous all over the Mediterranean, is another example of the pan-Mediterranean feel of Sardinian viniculture and grapes. *(Wine Searcher, 2020)*

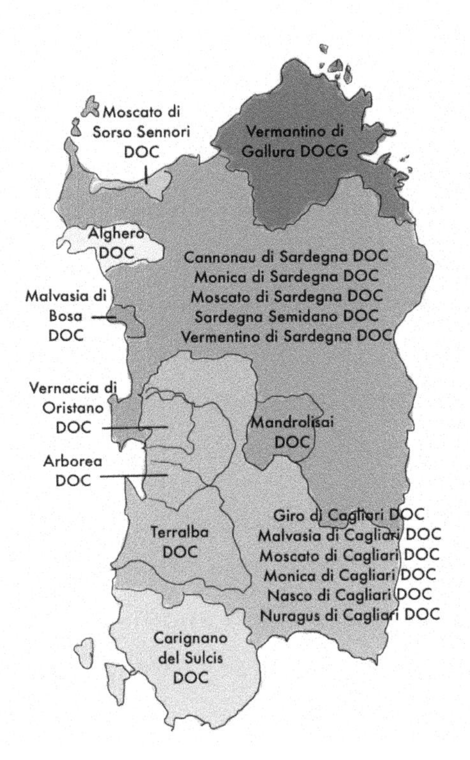

Fig 25. Sardinia Grape Map

Aside from the better-known grape varieties mentioned above, with their European influences but well-known names, the island also is home to a few obscure and fairly exclusive grape varieties, including the below:

- Torbato
- Semidano
- Niederra

- Nuragus
- Nasco
- Monica

Internally popular grapes from France, such as Cabernet Sauvignon, Merlot, Chardonnay and Sauvignon Blanc, are the new threat to Italian native grape varieties, and are being planted in ever-increasing numbers all over the country and with high success rates internationally. (*Wine Searcher, 2019*)

We all know them and we all drink them, but these foreign versions are not only ending up as dinner table wines; some of Italy's finest and most expensive wines are now made from these "foreign" varieties. (*Wine Searcher, 2019*)

This reflects a real change in trends, and an obvious example is the Super Tuscan Sassicaia from Bolgheri, which is predominantly made from Cabernet Sauvignon with around 15% Cabernet Franc.

A few more interesting wines to try:

A few more interesting wines of note now that we know more about native grapes and regions:

- Chiaretto; another name for rosé and produced in numerous Italian wine regions where it is most commonly a blend of red grapes. A great way to drink this mostly - Piemonte rosé is on one of the five hot summer days we get in England, or for the rest of Europe, any time during what I believe is called 'summer.'
- Ruché is an aromatic red grape that is indigenous to Piemonte as well, and can be found under the 'Ruché di Castagnole Monferrato DOCG' at its highest classification. But all versions of this wine are great spiced notes of pepper, mint and even cinnamon, and are balanced by floral aromas worthy of any sunny afternoon.
- Croatina (aka *Bonarda*) is a red wine with high levels of tannin and acidity, and the makings of a wonderful age-worthy wine to try. These wines - from Cisterna d'Asti, Collina Torinese, Colli Tortonesi, and Coste della Sesia primarily - are often labelled as "Bonarda" and deliver red berry fruit with a touch of residual sugar. One for the sweet-toothed and those looking to try something a bit different.

In wrapping up our grape regional tour, we have learned that Italy is responsible for producing some of the most beautiful varietal wine (primarily or entirely from one specific grape) we come across globally. But with so many native varieties growing throughout all 20 wine regions, we have covered the top few or standout unusual cases, as well as a few that share characteristics, to arm you with a sound understanding of this little fruit family - as we now move to Day 6 to tackle crossings and new trends.

SUMMARY OF DAY 5

Today we have learned that there truly are a few flagship grapes creating some of the most well-known wine expressions we now have in our vocabulary.

The most commonly planted grape in Italy is the Sangiovese, most famously used to make Chianti which we tried on Day 1 - a Tuscan wine named after the region in which it is produced.

This famed grape is generally known for bright red fruit flavours with plenty of acidity, and the Chianti variety is no exception.

We also celebrated Montepulciano d'Abruzzo after trying it on Day 4, made from the grape Montepulciano - the nearby Central Italian region to Tuscany.

This is a deeply coloured, full-bodied and rustic wine that from trying it should be celebrated with a slice of pizza on any given Italian holiday. In fact, book that right now.

In the North we looked at how the Barbera grape is the most planted red-grape variety, and is native to Piemonte - the North-Western region of Italy.

This dark-skinned grape generally produces superior wines with lower tannin and higher acidity, and we looked at these examples and the foods they complement.

Nearby in Veneto, Glera is undoubtedly another of Italy's most famous grape varieties, known otherwise to most as Prosecco. The Glera grape is exclusive to Italy and is the main ingredient for Italy's most celebrated sparkling wine brand.

So, if you can wrap your head around no more than ten of the most well-known native grapes we have covered today, you'll be able to walk into any Italian restaurant and hold your own, and certainly be able to choose wisely.

Study the Italian varietal table at the start of this chapter, and some fantastic examples of each grape family, and you'll be ready in no time for our penultimate day together to look at 'crossings.' (don't worry we will get to that tomorrow.)

DAY 5 WINE

Today we are going to try a grape we haven't explored much of yet, the Turbiana. It is a white grape that makes fruity wines, with flavours of its orchard terroir and stone fruits, *(Mama Blip, 2021)* and is used to make still dry, off-dry, and sparkling wines such as today's wine - 'Laguna, 100% Turbiana - Pratello Lombardy.'

Genetically similar to another more famous white grape, the Verdicchio, this is as close as we have got to doing this variety justice so far, since it is relatively rare entry-level and not as well-known.. yet. The traditional centre of Turbiana production is Lugana DOC close to Lake Garda in North-East Italy. *(Mama Blip, 2021)*

So let's get stuck into this fine example of a great Italian white - sold for a very reasonable £17.50. (US$21)

The producers are the Bertola family at the Pratello estate which occupies a favourable spot at altitude overlooking Lake Garda. The family planted the most suitable 66 hectares with vines in 2004; the rest of the land is given over to forest and cereal crops, *(Eat Vita, 2022)* and is another example of sustainable attention and patience to the land.

The vineyards have in fact been cultivated organically since planting, with excellent drainage and airflow that helps keep the grapes

healthy.

In 2016, the producers followed suit in a transition from certified organic viticulture to a charter of even more sustainable viticulture. With juices fermented in stainless steel tanks for ten days, then racked and aged for three months before bottling, once ready the result is delightful.

Pour into your glass and enjoy the moment of expressiveness on the nose (you'll be ready for more of this sort of tasting chat by Day 6 I promise) It has notes of citrus, apple and herbs. The palate will feel round and apricot-laden, but with a tautness that provides

an elegant finish.

What foods to pair it with?

Turbiano can range from youthful to off-dry, and gently rich - but the grape itself has a profile whatever the stage, which will pair well with lighter meats and poultry and salads. It is also the perfect match for risottos, fish and followed up with delicate desserts.

The following meat and fish go particularly well with this wine and keep things fairly simple on the cookery front:

- Charcuterie platters.
- Seafood with light sauces or in deep-fried batter.
- Seafood pasta.
- Game and poultry dishes.
- Light Asian and Indian cuisine.
- Oysters (maybe a tad exotic here but one to order out if Turbiano is on the menu)

On the awards front it has won the Gold Medal at the Sommelier Wine Awards 2019 among a few others, and we guess that many more trophies are on their way to their shelves… enjoy a fine example of Lombardy my friends, and on to our penultimate day together.

DAY 5 TAKE AWAY LESSON

Now, assuming you are looking to invest this new-found pleasure in wine, with a collection at-home as well, then I thought it was important to cover home storage for wine in these chapters. I have left this until slightly later as we are growing in confidence by now and these things hopefully feel more within reach than on Day 1?

I can speak from experience when I say that one of the great pleasures of learning about and enjoying wine is creating your home wine collection that is personal to your tastes. It is also one of the best things about owning your own house and choosing wine storage over kitchen cabinets but maybe that says more about me than anything.

When preserved correctly, wine can last for decades and be at its very best when it is - even growing in value and in quality. But it takes more than patience to do so and needs the space in your homes and in your lives. *(Masterclass, 2021)*

Here are some simple tips for storing wine effectively at home, without needing a cellar the size of your apartment:

- **Store wine at the proper temperature, and away from light and vibrations**

As we touched on even in Day 1's take away lesson - of all the factors influencing stored wine, temperature is the most important. Remember that the ideal temperature for long-term or short-term wine storage is around 55°F (13°C) and kept as stable as possible ideally in a dark room away from washers and dryers whose vibrations also interrupt the ageing process.

- **Store wine bottles horizontally on a wine rack**

For bottles with corks, be sure to store your wine horizontally on a wine rack. These do not have to be expensive or flashy, nor take up a lot of room (image below) Keeping wine on its side helps keep the cork moist which is important for longer term storage - and while it is not essential to keep screw top wine bottles on their sides as well, it is an efficient way to store your wines for maximum space and easy access, especially if you are looking to grow your collection.

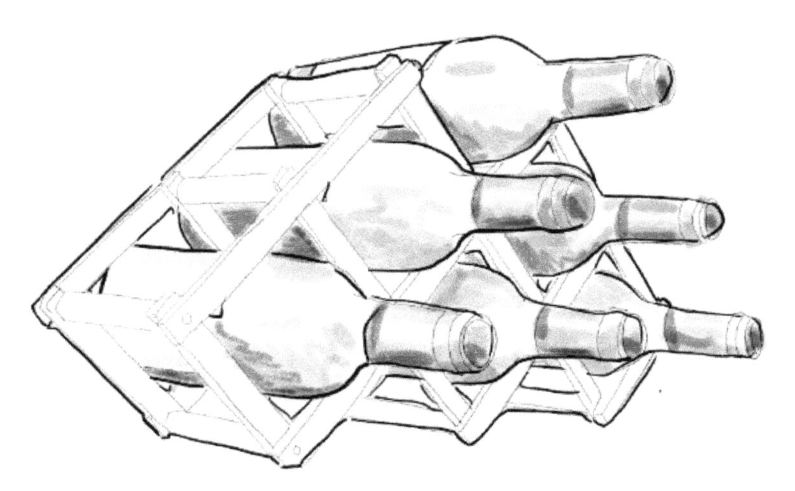

Fig 26. Wines in a wine rack

- **Store wine at the correct humidity**

At lower humidity levels, your corks can dry out and leave the wine vulnerable to the effects of oxygen, while higher humidity can cause labels to peel off the bottles. As a general rule, if you are lucky enough to actually have a cellar then 1) can I come over for dinner and 2) Try to keep it at 60 and 68 percent. For everyone else try to keep your kitchens or place of storage at a similar temperature as much as you can.

- **Store in a wine fridge if possible,**

I get it, it's not first on the list after a fridge and a washing machine when you move house, but where possible (if you're looking to do this seriously) then store wine in a wine fridge rather than a normal fridge. If you don't have a wine storage space that's consistently cool, dark, and the right humidity then this is even more essential. It also helps prevent cross-contamination from food odours - we all know what that week-old broccoli starts to smell like.

- **Serve at the right temperature**

As we touched upon when we were fresh out the blocks on Day 1's take away lesson as well - when preparing to serve a stored bottle to fellow wine enthusiasts (you are now those people), allow time for it to match the serving room temperature. This ensures a full expression of wine aroma and flavour that needs to be released before serving. A reminder of the approximate stats; red wine should be served chilled and just slightly below room temperature, approx between 58 and 65°F (about 12-19°C). Even older wines are held better at 61-65°F and younger wines on the colder end, while white sparkling wines and sweet whites should also be.

(Masterclass, 2021)

It is good to think of an investment in your wine storage, being an investment in your wine also. If you are starting to think about growing a wine collection and doing this properly at home, then you will need to invest in the appropriate storage and care of your new precious cargo. When preserved correctly, wine can last for decades and flourish in the comfort of your home, growing in both value and in quality, ready to make you proud.

GLOSSARY OF DAY 5 TERMS

Allochthonous - in this context; the grape "originated" from or is indigenous to where it is cultivated and so was not "imported"

Pergola system - The pergola is what we call a horizontal vine training system

DAY 6

CROSSINGS AND HYBRIDS

CROSSINGS

As we have explored over the past few days, Italy's grape varieties and their potential to clone and mutate depending on their terroir, speaks for the vast numbers of varieties found all over Italy.

The circumstances in which many grape varieties were created in the first place – be that spontaneous, intentional or otherwise – are not commonly known. *(Wine Searcher, 2018)* But what we do know is the generational ability of a grape type is extended even further if winemakers look to consciously reproduce positive characteristics. Like being able to choose your children for example - now there's an idea!

So what we call a 'viticultural clone,' (or just 'clone' as I have been using) strictly speaking is a vine that has been selected from an identical parent vine. This can be done deliberately to reproduce the parent characteristics, and then all clones are considered part of the same variety - hence many of the different expressions of the same grapes we discovered when looking at the impact of terroir.

Mutation is slightly different, but ends at the same result of a clone. Since no vineyard is subject to identical conditions, over time mutations will take place naturally (even without humans playing God and cloning them) and so in similar ways, you end up with genetic differences and characteristics that will be detectable over time.

Over time and repeated propagations of different vines, grapes from the same general DNA profile can end up being embraced as new, distinct varieties. *(Wine Searcher, 2018)* Sometimes mutation will even change the colour or size of the grape, or make other substantial changes to the original. However these are correctly described as the same variety but could be explained as a different 'expression' as I have also used until this point.

So, now we have set the scene to this point, we move to the next stage, and the meaning of a 'crossing' - this is a brand new grape variety which is created by the "cross-pollination of two varieties from the same species." *(Wine Searcher, 2018)*

In Piemonte in the 1930s, Professor Giovanni Dalmasso historically created several key crossings using Nebbiolo di Dronero, and the outcome has since been proven to be the Chatus variety, unrelated to Nebbiolo. *(Wine Searcher, 2018)*

These examples also include Albarossa, whose other parent is Barbera and has formed a new variety.

It is said that advances in clonal selection have the potential to improve and make better wines - but in all honesty *if something isn't broken...* right? We know the rest. Often you don't get the perfect clone, and it could lack either acidity for example, or fruit flavour. But by blending another clone that supplies that vibrancy you tend to get the perfect marriage - so, we find ourselves seeing wines created with multiple clones as the solution.

Not all crossings are created in a laboratory or research centre in later times, and indeed are not always necessarily intentional - the process may happen spontaneously in a vineyard.

In fact DNA profiling over the years has identified the parentage of many familiar varieties' with this being the case; in another example of Nebbiolo grapes for example, the Bubbierasco is a red Italian wine grape variety that is grown in the province of Cuneo also in the Piemonte region, and is a 'natural' crossing of the Nebbiolo with Bianchetta di Saluzzo, a white grape variety that has been historically grown around Saluzzo.

It is important to wrap up this definition and its examples by clarifying that a crossing is a unique combination of new genetic information, and it is that which makes it a new wine type.

Let's look at what is widely considered one of Italy's most successful crossings, and the implications this has on the types of wines consumers are starting to buy into.

'Manzoni Bianco' is not a native Italian grape, but a crossing between Riesling and Pinot Bianco (Pinot Blanc). *(Wine Scholar Guild, 2020)*

Considered a 'noble' crossing thanks to the quality of the wines that can be produced from it, Manzoni Bianco plantings have been gradually increasing thanks to winemakers who have begun to explore the true potential of the variety. When looking further into where this is being most adopted and where the variety flourishes, both Trentino and Veneto are the two principal regions, but it can also increasingly be found in smaller numbers in Alto Adige and Friuli. *(Wine Scholar Guild, 2020)*

Manzoni Bianco is an early to mid-ripening variety and in terms of its terroir it performs best on hillsides over clay soils. It is able to achieve high sugar levels while preserving its acidity. 'On the nose,' which yes we now say, it can be characterised by floral notes such as jasmine, as well as aromas of apples, stone fruits and hints of tropical fruit. *(Wine Scholar Guild, 2020)*

There are many other similar examples such as these - where a production almost 100 years ago has come full circle after a period of low yields, to a now extremely successful and celebrated crossing wine with increased attention on quality. We will look closely at other emerging wine types and trends in the following section…

HYBRIDS

Hybrids are the product of two or more different vitis species, and sometimes called 'interspecific crossings' or more widely these days as 'modern varieties.'

The original research into man-made hybrids began in the early 20th Century after the devastation caused by the phylloxera louse plague, *(Wine Searcher, 2018)* which we covered in the introduction - and how it set the scene for the new age of winemaking as a result.

Often the varieties resulting from that era show excellent resistance to fungal diseases for reasons mentioned above. An excellent early example of a hybrid from the 1930s is the 'Vidal' grape, whose parents were Ugni Blanc (the French name for Trebbiano Toscano) and Rayon d'Or (Seibel 4986) was developed by French viticulturist Jean-Louis Vidal with an intention of Cognac production, but the result was a new hybrid. *(Wine Searcher, 2020)*

Intentional or not, he didn't end up with a Cognac, but Vidal displayed an incredible tolerance for cold weather, and it now plays its role in being used in ice wine and sweet, late-harvest wines, and able to grow throughout colder regions like Canada and the USA and even Sweden. *(Wine Searcher, 2020)*

Due to the ongoing effects of climate change, which is far bigger than this book could ever dive into, even just on wine, vital research continues today more often as a means of dealing with its effects.

Out of necessity, the wine industry is looking at some hybrids making inroads into Italian regions more associated with vinifera varieties, to suit varying climate temperatures and altered conditions.

In the best article I have read on this topic - "Hybrid Grapes for a Sustainable Viticulture in South Italy" - by Antonia Boggia, she covers how a new sustainable approach to viticulture could be achieved by growing hybrid grape varieties inheriting tolerance/resistance characters from the wild vines. *(MDPI, 2021)*

The study proved Chambourcin was one of the most promising hybrid varieties, producing quality red wine and less interventions, and in terms of its parentage it found ancestry from vitis vinifera as a majority, followed by vitis berlandieri (about 28%), vitis rupestris (about 19%) and to a lesser extent other American wild vines. *(MDPI, 2021)*

In addition, this and other increasing hybrid research focuses on ecological concerns that are also part of the bigger climate change picture, and how we can reduce the use of chemical sprays and impact on the planet in our vineyards. The above compelling study concluded that considering the environmental benefits of the hybrid include decreasing the chemicals usage in viticulture (preventing contamination of the soils) and cheap vine propagation resistant to louse. *(MDPI, 2021)* In summary, growing Chambourcin and other resistant grapevines in South Italy in particular, says this study, could lead to environmentally and economically sustainable production of quality wine with a greater respect for habitats and aquatic life. *(MDPI, 2021)*

However, the downside to this direction is that wines made from hybrid varieties tend to retain some of the less desired traits of the non-vinifera species, and can sometimes be associated with musky and less attractive aromas.

In addition, red hybrids are often found to be high in acidity but low in tannin, again seemingly less desirable. As well as prompting the creation of many of these hybrid grape varieties, the Phylloxera outbreak we covered in the introduction, also led to the widespread use of grafted vines, i.e. rootstocks from American vine species which were joined to a piece of Vitis vinifera vine. *(Wine Searcher, 2018)*

And lastly, the hybrid does not have to have a vitis vinifera parent (I will explain why below) - any more complicated detail than that I think I would lose myself let alone trying to follow along.

But it is to say that the lines get blurred when you get any deeper into this topic, and for the sake of a basic understanding of these definitions and a few examples, I think you are all set.

EMERGING WINE STYLES

Despite the fear of even touching the hugely daunting topic of climate change, it cannot be ignored in the development of changing wine styles and emerging new combination varieties.

According to the 2021 changes made by the Official Journal of the European Union, part of a wider revision of previous regulations for common quality, member states can now use "vine varieties belonging to vitis vinifera as well as hybrids containing both vitis vinifera and non-vinifera genetic material from vine species of American and Asian origin." *(Decanter, 2021)*

The EU's decision came as a direct response to the challenges posed by climate change, thus helping the European winegrowing industry become more sustainable *(Decanter, 2021)* and take the direction needed to thrive and be embraced.

Indeed, as well as sustainability, a number of hybrid varieties benefit from a higher resistance and resilience to common diseases such as downy and powdery mildew, meaning that the vineyards require little to no treatments, be these chemical pesticides or organic-approved copper spraying. (*Wine Searcher, 2018)*

As we looked at briefly on Day 3, Abruzzo in Central Italy is today also gearing towards producing more quality-driven wines with a notable increase in quaint, sustainable and boutique wineries. One of the pioneers of this style is Gianni Masciarelli, whose winery is part of a new generation driving the marked improvements in wine quality in this region and beyond.

Gianni's story is a sad one, but with a happy ending - phew.

Intensely innovative for his day, Gianni increased the density of the Trebbiano vine plantings - reducing bunch size in order to concentrate the flavour in individual grapes. This process helped transform Trebbiano d'Abruzzo table wine from its place as a low-end 'generic' wine enjoyed since the Roman times, to a far higher quality buttery wine. *(Forbes, 2017)*

In his lifetime, Gianni transformed his winery 'Villa Gemma' into one that eventually produced 650,000 bottles a year and of a markedly more celebrated variety.

Sadly, Gianni was only in his early 50's when he died unexpectedly, leaving his Abruzzo wine empire in the hands of his Serbian widow, Marina Cvetic. *(Forbes, 2017)*

She was raising three children and the reality is that she faced the very real prospect of closing the winery, or taking the helm of their expanding wine empire. She chose the latter, and today, she and her daughter Miriam work together to run the property and since Gianni's passing, they have guided the empire to increased wine production, and the incorporation of tourism (including the operation hilltop castle—Castello di Semivicoli) *(Forbes, 2017)*

A combined effort of what Gianni had achieved decades ago with his intuitiveness, and Marina's great leadership since his passing, has led to the creation of a diversified product line that is sustainable and built on a family empire.

It includes grappa and olive oils and the expansion of a distribution network that caters to products by other companies' support. *(Forbes, 2017)* She has received several awards for her business acumen and leadership, and honours those family members who have gone before her, including winemaker husband Gianni, as well her own grandfather in his vineyard, to celebrate a more quality-driven wine that we see today. *(Forbes, 2017)*

Now, let's look at other specific emerging styles of the wine world that are creating a stir here and now…

SPARKLING WINES

We are going to cover sparkling wines produced in different parts of Italy. Here's everything you need to know about my current recommended top 4 - from their grape varieties to their taste and characteristics.

Firstly, we can't not start with:

- Prosecco

The sparkling white wine famous the world over, made from Glera grapes (at least 85%) and the go-to wine for celebratory occasions and the crux of any drinks reception.

The DOC classification for Prosecco includes three styles: Frizzante, Spumante, and still Prosecco. *(Vino Vest, 2022)*

Prosecco is made in the Veneto and Friuli Venezia Giulia regions of Italy, and can be brut, dry, extra dry and demi-sec. The grape gives the wine the flavours of melon, apple & pear and honeysuckle, among other aromas. (Vino Vest, 2022)

My recommendation for an excellent Prosecco is (rather snobbily) a DOCG wine from Treviso called Asolo Prosecco DOCG. Most production here is oriented towards spumante (fully sparkling) styles, which are the only ones that can be labelled as Superiore if you're looking for the whole hoorah on the bubbles front. *(Taste Atlas, 2022)*

Fig 27. Map of Prosecco region

Now, a variation on this that is only fairly recent in its official recognition:

- Prosecco rosé

Here come the girls! Granted it may still be fairly feminine in its appreciation, since 2020 the production of Prosecco rosé has been officially approved by the Italian government and it's a drink you won't see missing at a girls night.

The wine can be made with Glera and Pinot Noir (Pinot Nero) grape varieties, with a maximum of 10-15% of Pinot Noir as additional grapes.

It has to be produced using the Charmat-Martinotti method which means the last 60 days takes place in pressurised tanks. *(Taste Atlas, 2022)*

The decision to approve official rosé versions has been a long time coming, and it is now expected that more than 30 million bottles of Prosecco rosé will be produced annually. *(Taste Atlas, 2022)* This only approved for Prosecco DOC, but with many great options (yes I've had a few hen evenings myself thank you) I recommend the below:

- 2019 Pizzolato Prosecco DOC Rosé Brut (US$19)
- 2019 Valdo Marca Oro Prosecco DOC Rosé Brut (US$15)

- 2019 Voga Prosecco DOC Rosé Extra Dry (US$13)

Next up.. (and working our way through the big names first of all)

- Lambrusco

Lambrusco is a sparkling red wine from the Emilia-Romagna region of Northern Italy and can range from a dry to a sweet wine. There are five major Lambrusco DOCs of which I recommend the below two as must-tries:

- Lambrusco Reggiano
- Lambrusco Mantovano

Furthermore, Lambrusco di Sambora is my particular favourite; a high-quality Lambrusco produced from a namesake grape variety grown in Modena and the village of Sorbara.

The region was awarded DOC status in 1970 and has been known to produce excellent fragrant, red and rosé sparkling wines as well. *(Taste Atlas, 2022)*

It is also worth noting that Riunite Lambrusco is a red, sweet example which is one of the most cherished drinks in the USA, so not to forget about that for our American friends - it has its place in a lot of hearts for its forest berry flavours and a fizzy sweetness. According to the Italian Wine & Food Institute in New York, Lambrusco remains the number two imported wine in the U.S. after Pinot Grigio. *(Wine Magazine, 2010)*

And finally for my recommended sparkling wine, a nod to what is widely regarded as the finest Italian sparkling:

- Franciacorta

Franciacorta is made using the same method as Champagne and Cava. It is produced with a typical blend of Chardonnay, Pinot Bianco and Pinot Nero and comes in standard white form as well as Franciacorta Satèn - made only with Chardonnay and Pinot Bianco grape - and Franciacorta Rosé made with at least 25% Pinot Nero. *(Taste Atlas, 2022)*

This variety of sparkling makes an excellent pairing for a wide range of dishes, from pasta and seafood dishes to cheese and charcuterie.

ORANGE WINES

Now onto the trend of orange wines, which I first tried when I lived in Australia in 2017 and honestly always hoped would catch on.

Having somewhat of a Renaissance with maybe exactly the type of demographic I fit into, orange wine has rightfully shown that it is a trend here to stay, even if not in huge numbers yet.

But gradually, bottles are appearing alongside more familiar red, white and rose offerings, everywhere from on-trend 'natural' wine bars to supermarket shelves. *(The Independent, 2022)*

Fig 28. Orange Wine

In essence, it is produced with white wine grapes but vinified as though they were red wines. Everyone keeping up so far? This method results in skin-contact white wines with grapes which are fermented in their skins and then yeast for up to a few months.

The wine then develops in a completely different way: aromatic substances and proteins change the final product totally in terms of visual and even textural points of view. *(Eataly, 2022)* As for the orange hue, with shades of amber that vary according to the structure of the wine, this varies even further if the wines are finished in wood casks. In Italy, you may hear some of these wines called "ramato," or amber, for their distinctive colours.

Most orange winemaking in Italy can be found in the North - East, along the border of Slovenia in Friuli-Venezia Giulia, and also nearby Northern regions Campania and Emilia Romagna.

In Friuli-Venezia Giulia you will find orange wines produced with the native grapes of the region, some of these new to you as we haven't dived as deep into this regions' varieties yet - but they include Sauvignon Vert (Friulano), Ribolla Gialla and Pinot Grigio

Our pick of the bunch (sorry, no pun intended) are the below distinctive and punchy orange offerings: (and by the way there are all organic so cheers to that)

- Baglio Antico Bianco 2021

This is an excellent value for money, entry-level orange wine. It has a rich, pithy fruit character with ginger, spices and more - a great place to start trying skin-contact white wine at £16 (US$20).

- Denavolo Dinavolino 2020

Denavolo is the project of Giulio Armani, winemaker for La Stoppa in Emilia Romagna. It has heady, floral notes and tannins La Stoppa wines are known for, *(Wayward Wines, 2022)* but is more modestly-priced and the exciting orange colour - we are sold.

It is the Malvasia grape that comes through the most, and you get orange blossom, grapefruit and limes from this, whilst the Marsanne grape gives off apricot and tea-like notes. *(Wayward Wines, 2022)*

The grapes are harvested fairly late and at full maturity, and the result is a great orange wine for a very reasonable £23 (US$28)

- La Distesa Nur 2020

At a slightly steeper £27 (US$33), we promise you the care and attention of the Corrado Dottori family make it worth stepping it up a gear in the world of orange wine. The family has tended vines in San Michele near the town of Cupramontana in the Marche region for three generations. *(Wayward wines, 2022)*

The vines sit at about 320 metres above sea level, in perfect terroir conditions for the Verdicchio grape. In this exciting wine you will find aromas of peas, alfalfa and from this earnest grower, the resulting wines are amongst Italy's finest.

QUALITY ROSATI / ROSÉ WINES

Having already explored the sparkling version of pink, the wider wine category of generic rosé is the fastest growing wine category when looking at emerging trends in the rest of the world.

In 2017 for example, the consumption of rosé grew by roughly 50%, compared with 4% of wine growth in general, and it hasn't slowed much since then. *(Forbes, 2018)*

The love of rosé seems to be a summer-must, and means it has serious potential for continued rapid growth as we enter longer and warmer summers. There is interestingly no generally accepted definition of what constitutes a rosé wine, other than the obvious that it incorporates some of the colour of a red wine.

More accurately (and perhaps helpfully) rosés tend to be low in tannins, even when they are darker colored, and are normally noticeably fruit forward, with crisp acidity and lighter on the palate than a classic red. *(Forbes, 2018)*

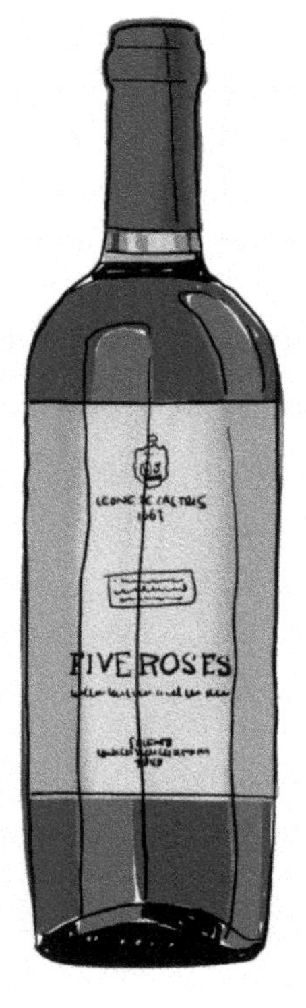

Fig 29. Rose Wine

Even with these qualifications, however, the distinction between a light red wine which we will get to shortly, and a rosé, can be rather tricky to define and are somewhat arbitrary. A rosé can, however, be considered more as a style of wine rather than a wine of a particular colour if that is helpful as a rule. *(Forbes, 2018)*

This is because rosés are generally produced either; by skin contact, by saignée or by blending and the less time with contact with the grape skins, the light the colour produced.

Despite a long tradition of making high-quality rosé wines, Italian production at home and domestic consumption of rosé wines has been falling since 2000, and it is not the Italian versions of rosés making it to export for demand in the United States and beyond. *(Forbes, 2018)*

Italy has three main rosé producing areas, and with a distinctive style and in high demand in the wine world which is not yet being met - this is either to savour the status of the wine or it just happens to be Italy's best kept secret still.

In the northeast, the principal rosé producing area is the region around Lake Garda - where I visited a few weeks ago. On the eastern side it is known as Chiaretto di Bardolino, from the Italian word 'chiara,' meaning clear, *(Forbes, 2018)* relating to its light colour and refreshing taste.

The type is most typically from a blend of Rondinella and Corvina grapes, and sometimes Morilano *(Forbes, 2019)* with notes of fresh citrus, grapefruit and oranges with tangerine, as well as red fruits.

Chiaretto can be produced in any one of 16 villages along the eastern shore of Lake Garda and I tried many excellent varieties. Of those in restaurants and sold locally as well as available in the UK and the USA, I would recommend:

- Poggio delle Grazie, Bardolino Chiaretto DOC 2017
- Vigneti Villabella, Bardolino Chiaretto DOC 2016

Legend has it that Chiaretto was first produced in 1896, yet it wasn't until 1968 that Chiaretto from Bardolino was awarded DOC status in recognition of its quality and tradition, and arguably only in the recent decade of the rosé trend that it is being rightfully celebrated and enjoyed.

The western side of Lake Garda is in Lombardy - still producing Chiaretto and part of the same region.

Since 2015, a specific DOC for Chiaretto in this subzone has been designated: Riviera del Garda Classico Chiaretto. *(Forbes, 2018)* There are 10 villages in this DOC that can produce Chiaretto - made with Gropello grapes or with blends of Gropello, Marzemino, Barbera or Sangiovese.

These are also dry examples, with pronounced flavours of strawberries and other red fruits. The pronounced strawberry aroma is the real marker for rosé from the

Riviera del Garda. *(Forbes, 2018)* A good example of this fruity version from the Lombardy area I would recommend is the below:

- Pasini San Giovanni Valtènesi Chiaretto, Riviera del Garda Classico DOC 2017

The second major rosé producing region in Italy is Abruzzo, and the expression from this region - the 'Cerasoulo di Abruzzi' - was the first rosé wine in Italy to achieve DOC status. Rather unusually, this version can be aged for years, and its name comes from the Italian for 'cherry' - hence its cherry colour, tone and flavour. It also features aromas of other red fruits including cranberry, strawberry and raspberry.

These wines can be deeply colored and richer, and almost appear like a red wine that is chilled. *(Forbes, 2018)* A great Abruzzo version I can highly recommend is:

- Codice Citra, Cerasoulo d'Abruzzo DOC, Ferzo 2017

The third major rosé region is Puglia, which we have studied in detail for its other varieties and specialities. This is one of Italy's warmest regions in the heel of the Italian boot, and sits aside the Adriatic and Ionian Seas.

The terroir here consists of rich and fertile soils, and as such the rosés (or rosatos as they are known locally) are produced from Bombino Nero grapes which thrive in these conditions, with blends of Negroamaro and Malvasia Nera.

There is also a Primitivo di Manduria rosé, which as explored in the previous chapter is considered a biotype of Zinfandel. *(Forbes, 2018)* Bombino Nero is used to produce light, pink colored rosés in the Castel Del Monte DOC.

The skins of this grape type don't have much colour to them, so even with the extended contact the resulting wine is still a very light pink.

The added Negroamaro, either with Malvasia Nera and sometimes Primitivo, is used in the rosé wines of the Salice Salento area of Puglia - these are darker with a note of almond and clay. *(Forbes, 2018)* Puglian examples of excellent rosés made with these grape combinations, are as below:

- Castel Del Monte Bombino Nero DOCG, Pungirosa 2017 (mentioned above) and;
- Candido, Salice Salentino Rosato DOC, Le Pozzelle 2017, 750 ml

All in all, Italian rosés represent a relatively untapped long-standing wine-making tradition in Italy that has not yet witnessed the same growth in export demands as other European countries. It has received little recognition despite their outstanding quality and value for money, and a sophisticated selection of wines that surpasses any other rosé producing country.

Ready to explore the world of Italian rosés? I would suggest making one of these three regions your next holiday destination and go straight to the source. Salute.

AGE-WORTHY WHITES

While Italian reds still soak up much of the wine world's attention, as we have discovered together throughout the course of this book, there are without doubt many outstanding Italian whites that deserve consideration, and many which have their own story to tell about improving even further with age.

Certain Italian white wines, which can often improve dramatically after a decade or more of ageing, show complexity beyond the first layer of bright and refreshing flavours *(Italian Wine Girl, 2022)* which overlook the qualities achieved with time.

The ageability of white wine is dependent on acid and sugar. In their youth, when age-worthy white wines have an abundance of acid which is so predominant they are one-dimensional wines with a bitter finish and a lack of sugar.

When you give these wines the gift of time and consequently oxidation, these elements balance themselves out and release further flavours and smells. *(Italian Wine Girl, 2022)*

It is strange that there is a lack of standard process for aging Italian white wines,when it is so readily accepted for French whites for example. If it was, we would be looking at the same quality of aged whites, but at a fraction of the cost. Here is a list of varieties and styles that only get better with age, and can stay up to 10-15 years in the cellar:

- Verdicchio Riserva

Simpler Verdicchio wines can certainly be enjoyed young, but the Riserva version deserves patience. After approximately 10 years of ageing these wines enter an revolutionised phase and the grapes become larger, broader and more structured on the palate. The fruity flavours become more exotic and the longer you give them to the 20 years mark, even better.

- Carricante from Sicily

Sicily is being celebrated for other reasons more closely associated with ts better-known reds, which we will explore shortly, but I wanted to share an excellent example of an age-worthy white from here too.

Benanti's 'Pietra Marina' is a savoury, almost saline-flavoured wine, and this is in fact part of its appeal *(New York Times, 2016)* Depending on the vintage, since it ages fantastically, Pietra Marina, can be rich and concentrated, and with time increasingly takes on a kerosene quality reminiscent of an aged Riesling. *(New York Times, 2016)*

But it's better. It never loses its succulence and balance, and I dare you not to love this.

Excitingly, there are far more lesser-known, rightfully trending, varieties of whites that are breaking the mould for similar reasons and moving towards a new found appreciation; all of which are worth seeking out.

A few examples I have chosen in this hugely serious mission to present you with only the best, that can also age brilliantly, include the below:

- Timorasso

Timorasso is rightly considered one of Piemonte's most exciting grapes, and is an ancient high-quality type, rescued by the dynamic producer Walter Massa (Vigneti Massa) *(Wine Scholar Guild, 2020)*

In recent years, its potential has attracted winemakers from outside its original terroir of Colli Tortonesi, Piemonte, and now includes top Barolo and Barbaresco producers such as Vietti and Roagna.

Timorasso ages very well and is at its best after at least a few years' of bottle ageing. What to look for? It usually comes under the Colli Tortonesi DOC label. *(Wine Scholar Guild, 2020)*

Now more than ever there is a growing awareness that Timorasso may possess a greater ability to age and achieve complexity - and finally it is being valued for its true age-worthy potential. *(The Italian Wine Girl, 2022)*

- Pallagrello Bianco

Pallagrello Bianco is more of a fine example of re-discovered varieties in the region of Campania - more specifically, the province of Caserta in North - West.

Much like Timorasso, it needed bringing back in the 20th Century and general attention; this time by Giuseppe Mancini, current owner of the Terre del Principe estate, who also rejuvenated two other forgotten and distinctive red grapes as now celebrate, Pallagrello Nero and Casavecchia. *(Wine Scholar Guild, 2020)*

It is known as a fertile, mid-ripe variety, with aromas that include apple, stone fruits and honey. Plantings of Pallagrello Bianco are still small and limited, and for now there are no DOCs dedicated to wines based on the grape, so a tip would be to look for those labelled under the Terre del Volturno IGT or Campania IGT *(Wine Scholar Guild, 2020)* and drink this slightly aged if you wish, or don't wait at all, it will still taste great.

NEW REDS AND LIGHT REDS

When it comes to light-bodied reds you can find easy-drinking, perfumed reds from right across Italy, and its varied climate and geography means it can produce wines in a variety of styles - now excelling in lighter versions.

Ignoring Lambrusco for now since we've covered it in this sparkling wines section, let's deep dive into light reds in all their glory. Piedirosso for example, is the second most-planted grape variety in Campania, Southern Italy, but it is relatively unknown as it's usually blended with other varieties. *(Decanter, 2021)*

Aglianico Piedirosso is a uniquely Italian blend of the two red wine grapes of Campania in southern Italy, used to great effect individually in light red wines such as Aglianico del Vulture and Capri Rosso. *(Wine Searcher, 2022)*

Food matches for Aglianico Piedirosso wines include aubergine-based dishes, duck and beef. Here is a couple of the best of the rest:

- La Tunella, Pinot Nero, Friuli, Colli Orientali 2017
- GB Burlotto, Dolcetto d'Alba, Piemonte 2019

Looking further, as mentioned when we looked at the Carricante grape, Sicily is the new face of Italy especially where 'good value' everyday red wines are concerned.

Thanks to the hard work of vintners on the island, such as Donnafugata, Cusumano, Benanti and Feudo Montoni, it is gradually shedding its image as a producer of bulk, cheap wine and is reinventing itself as a place of quality production instead. *(Wine Enthusiast, 2010)*

A great example here as the times change to embrace this new status of Sicilian wines, is the below variety:

- Nero d'Avola

This grape's expression of 'Planeta Santa Cecilia.' *(Wine Enthusiast, 2010)* is a wholesome, pure red wine, and shares aromas of mature fruit, blackberry, herbs and pistachio, and shows the untapped potential of this extraordinary terroir on the island. *(Wine Enthusiast, 2010)*

And most famously, a variety we have given a great deal of time to already but one Italy's most famous grapes:

- Nebbiolo

Again, known for its use in Barolo and Barbaresco, Nebbiolo is the well-known light red variety in Italy, and produces high tannin, light red wine that will dry out the insides of your cheeks - in a good way if that sounds distressing.

It smells like roses, clay, cherries as well as savoury red currant flavours among many others. *(Wine Folly, 2022)*

While recently having covered whites that age brilliantly, let's not forget that Barolo in particular, made in the most traditional way, is one of the slowest-maturing wines in the world and will easily flourish with four decades in bottle. *(Jancis Robinson, 2022)*

Fig 30. Cantine Pupillo, Sicily.

Nebbiolo has also been planted more recently in newly-created zones of Albugnano, Canavese, as well as the hills around Novara and on the banks of the Sesia river. Gattinara, Ghemme and Sizzano are all new varieties of wines that are predominantly dependent on Nebbiolo and forming part of a new generation of the grape family. *(Jancis Robinson, 2022)*

I want to take more time to look in depth at Carema as a light-red variety using Nebbiolo; a perfect wine for those seeking the litheness of a Barolo, but from a new and much-sought-after tiny growing appellation that deserves attention.

Tiny but impressive. This unique terroir is a great example of one producing fantastic high-altitude Nebbiolo - in the midst of a renaissance with new winegrowers reclaiming abandoned vineyards and developing them into forward-thinking ones producing wines of distinction. *(Decanter, 2022)*

It is also a great example as we look at the direction of viticulture into the future and how to sustain it, of 'heroic viticulture' - which is terracing the vines against gravity basically.

Carema's remoteness; the high-altitude terracing, and defined minimal infrastructure, *(Decanter, 2022)* makes it a challenging but rewarding place to produce excellent wine. Nebbiolo di Carema *(Vivino, 2022)* as it is easily called, is available for a very reasonable £23 and I have no doubt you will enjoy it.

NATURAL, ORGANIC AND BIODYNAMIC WINES

In looking at Italian natural, organic and biodynamic wines, I can only serve to tell you about the wines I have read about or tried, that are produced in harmony with nature and as an expression of their territory.

As such, I will provide a map of winemakers in a sense, to discover those who promote a new ecological awareness in viticulture - and are rightfully gaining recognition and respect for doing so.

Let's look at the difference between these three terms.. 'Organic wines' are certified according to a European regulation.

In the vineyard there must be production of organic grapes, grown without the help of synthetic chemicals or genetically modified organisms. And in the cellar, vinification is carried out using only the oenological products and processes authorised by regulations. *(Vino-Bio, 2022)*

Fig 31. European label for Organic Wine

Our favourite Italian winery in the organic spectrum is Mont'Albano, founded in 1985 in Friuli Venezia Giulia by Mauro Braidot who converted 5 hectares of vineyard to organic production. Thanks to its philosophy it grew quickly and in 1998 expanded to form Mont'Albano a limited partnership company. It also egan processing grapes grown by other producers, provided by trusted regional producers who respect the strict guidelines in order to proudly put its brand on its products. *(Vino-Bio, 2022)*

Moving on to the meaning of 'biodynamic' wine, and how that differs to organic - the three principles of biodynamics are as follows:

- Maintain the fertility of the earth, freeing the nutrients within it;
- Make plants healthy so they can withstand diseases, pests and other threats, and;
- Produce foods of the highest quality possible.

(Vino-Bio, 2022)

(For a more in-depth look at the characteristics of biodynamic agriculture, see the website of the Association for Biodynamic Agriculture.)

As visited when championing fine orange wines, I want to revisit the La Distesa Nur 2020 at this point to celebrate the wider biodynamic efforts of the Dottori family at the helm of this wonderful winery.

As we know, the resulting orange wine (and wider suite of wines) are certainly something to celebrate, but the truth is the production efforts are the true joy in this story. Biodiversity is both championed and cherished here, as as briefly mentioned in yesterday's chapter you will detect everything in here from fava beans to alfalfa in between the rows of vines, providing the most diverse terroir in which the vines can thrive. *(Wayward Wines, 2022)*

Not only that but the raw materials for the biodynamic preparations used and the preparation of the vineyard are all applaudable, done with a conscience and a care for the land. The focus is on attaining pure fruit through organic viticulture and low harvest yields. *(Wayward Wines, 2022)* A blend of Trebbiano, Malvasia and Verdicchio grapes are fermented on skins for two weeks and aged for a further year and a half in barrels and stainless steel before the end result, and all of this under the watchful eye of the third generation of Corrado Dottori's family. It is bottled unfiltered, with no additives, and possesses natural aromatics of citrus, herbs and spices. *(Wayward Wines, 2022)*

The finest examples of the end results, beyond the orange variety, are as follows:

- La Distesa 'Terre Silvate' Marche Bianco IGT for approximately £15 and;
- La Distesa Gli Eremi, Verdicchio dei Castelli di Jesi Classico Riserva DOCG for £25

And finally, 'natural wines.' Now, this is as classically confusing as you have probably come to expect of Italian wine classification systems - in essence, I need to clarify that there is no defined, agreed definition of 'natural wine,' and furthermore, the term does not exclude the characteristic of "naturalness" of organic and biodynamic wines.

Instead it seemingly refers to a broader set of the actual producers who might not undergo a certification but refuse to use chemical products of synthesis and to intervene at cellar level with invasive practices. *(Vino-Bio, 2022)*

What is agreed by this group certainly, is that producing wine in a natural way means acting in full respect of the territory; the vine and natural cycles. It is also understood that natural wines limit the use of invasive and toxic agents in both the vineyard and the cellar. (*Gourmet Hunter, 2022)*

They also apparently don't give you a headache which should be universally appreciated and never underestimated.

My pick of the best natural wines and ready to test that theory are:

- Cascina Travijn Vino Rosso 2019

This is a fruity young aged red wine from Piemonte region, made from a blend of Barbera and Freisa grapes.

- Ombretta Rosso 2020

This is another young red from the Costadilà winery in Veneto - and a blend of Merlot and Cabernet Franc grapes. With only 11% alcohol maybe that's where the assured xero headache comes in, it's practically harmless.

(Gourmet Hunters, 2022)

I hope that under the different definitions, I have managed to give you a selection of some of the best Italian bottles of natural, organic and biodynamic wines - all of which can certainly be agreed are made with ethical attention to production and minimal intervention and respect for the land and grape.

Fig 32. Italian vineyard

Antonio Capaldo, President of leading Campania firm 'Feudi di San Gregorio' puts it rather perfectly when he says that "rather than make wines that taste like they could be made anywhere, we want to make wines that express native grapes and our unique terroir." *(Wine Mag, 2022)*

Winemakers such as Capaldo are ensuring they use less "invasive cellar techniques" *(Wine Mag, 2022)* and join the effort to produce more ethical and clean wines as the world changes the way it consumes.

The attention of where wine comes and the new plight to interfere less with its journey, is evident in the above stories and will warm every wine-lovers' heart.

NEW WAVE ITALIAN WINES

As mentioned briefly when covering the age-worthy versions of whites - giving them the time and patience we'd expect for reds - my money is on Italy's new breed of white wines soon getting the attention they deserve in reputation.

Today, we can see whites from far beyond just the cooler regions, boasting the complexities and minerali-ties often celebrated only in these climates.

The 'new wave' of wines is down to the winemakers (as is always the case of course) now focusing on native grapes, which have adapted to the region's climate over hundreds of years, and changing to accommodate, as we have seen earlier, to suit their terroirs. Here's a list of my best of the best.

- Feudi di San Gregorio 2012.

Made from organically-grown grapes, this boasts a floral fragrance of chamomile with citrus and mineral flavours. Priced at $37 but worth every penny.

- Ciro Picariello 2012

Delicious and linear, with aromas of white flowers, grapefruit and nectarine. Priced at $23 if you're looking for a more every day version.

- D'Antiche Terre 2012

This is a crisp wine with nectarine, peach and a punch of acidity and almond. This is approximately $19 as we get even more well-valued for an excellent variety.

While on new age whites, I read an interesting article from a regional writer in Sussex, in the UK, suggesting there might be a newly designated quality Italian wine region called Pignoletto, that would soon be **the** 'new wave' Italian wine in the UK - where I am based if anyone is interested.. In the interest of transparency the article is from 2017 and since I would argue it isn't yet rivalling the popularity of Pinot Grigio, that if the article was meant as a question of 'will it be next..' then I suggest the answer is, at the very least, not yet.

But Pignoletto as a wine has been around for a long time and is well respected by the locals of the Emilia Romagna region *(Sussex World, 2017)* and I agree there is certainly the space for it to join this 'new wave.'

There is room for everyone. I mean, it's what we tell our children in the playground even if we don't mean it. But in this case I might... Pignoletto is made from the Grechetto Gentile grape, and in order to protect the authenticity of the wines made from it (near Bologna mainly) a new DOC was created called Pignoletto, centred on the small village of Monteveglio. *(Sussex World, 2017)*

It is available in fully sparkling (spumante) or semi-sparling (frizzante) as well as a still wine, nearly always dry and with a higher alcohol content than the other fizzy versions, at 13%.

The DOC regulations governing Pignoletto wines allow for some other grape varieties to be used in conjunction with the Grechetto as standard for the DOC classification. In this case the most common is international Chardonnay, with another being the local variety, Barbera.

In the case of the latter, the colourful skins are eliminated at a very early stage in the wine-making process, so that only the white juice remains. *(Sussex World, 2017)* My favourites?

- Pignello Pignoletto Frizzante 2020 (not yet in the UK much but some buyers have it and only £10 (US$12) approximately if you can manage to get your hands on it)
- Cevico Pignoletto Frizzante Colli Imola 2018 (similar in style and price but completely fabulous as well)
- 'Tenuta Monteveglio' Pignoletto Colli Bolognesi DOCG, 2020 - approximately £17 (US$20)

All things considered, I am jumping on this bandwagon of Pignoletto being one to watch - is it because I have recently seen the sparkling versions making new appearances on the shelves of UK supermarkets? Not at all. I am rooting for the still versions anyway…

SUMMARY OF DAY 6

So, looking back on a big day of learning, we have covered crossings and hybrid wine varieties, as well as learned the differences between the two. We covered how the circumstances in which many grape varieties were created in the first place can be spontaneous, intentional or otherwise – and in many cases are still arguable. But what we did confirm is the ability of a grape type is extended even further if there is a conscious reproduction of positive characteristics.

The meaning of a 'crossing' to take away from today, is a brand new grape variety which is created by the cross-pollination of two varieties from the same species.

We moved on to emerging wine styles - and the continued, growing popularity of sparkling Italian wines, including the famous Prosecco, its closely related Prosecco rosé, and on to Lambrusco and finally Franciacorta - as well as my recommendations.

The world of orange wine was covered, and in general you just need to take away that they tend to be grown in the Friuli-Venezia Giulia region and nearby Northern regions Campania and Emilia Romagna. Our pick of the best included Baglio Antico Bianco 2021 and Denavolo Dinavolino 2020 if you've only got time for a quick scribble down of a few names before the next online wine order.

Today we have covered the seemingly huge world of wider rosés, and their overwhelming popularity worldover. Yet with Italy not yet at the forefront of these exports and still relatively untapped as a market in this regard, I could share some little gems that you won't find in most people's shopping basket - unless they're recently home from an Italian jaunt. Such as Castel Del Monte Bombino Nero DOCG and Candido, Salice Salentino Rosato DOC.

We dabbled in age-worthy white wines, and those which have their own story to tell about improving with up to a decade or more of ageing, show complexity beyond the first layer of bright and refreshing flavours, such as Timorasson and Carricante grapes, which also shares its glory in being from the same region as the new lighter reds on the scene Sicily.

Moving onto these, we looked at how Piedirosso for example, is the second most-planted grape variety in Campania but is still fairly unknown as it's usually blended with other varieties. *(Decanter, 2021)*

And finally, I shared the difference between organic wines (certified according to a European regulation), natural and Biodynamic wines - and the implications these have towards a new wave of conscious winemaking, as well as a selection of some of the best Italian bottles made with ethical attention to production a respect for the land.

Italy's new breed of wines with this kind of personalised, organic attention are starting to get the attention they deserve.

The 'new wave' of wines this leads us to, is down to the winemakers now focusing on native grapes, which have adapted to the region's climate over hundreds of years.

What has also become clear as we wrap up a day of changing wine styles, is that Italy is being forced to look for new ways of winegrowing, whether it likes it or not, due to the huge impacts of climate change and the world we live in.

In 2020 for example, temperatures fell below freezing during the Spring period in April, something that never previously happened, while in Veneto 300 kilometres to the East, there was significantly more rain than usual in the same months. *(Syngenta Group, 2022)*

This weather and its impact on the harvests, places extreme pressure on the Italian wine industry, and we cross our fingers that the answers to this, such as hybrid variations and new, sustainable exports, are not in vain to save it in time.

DAY 6 WINE

Our penultimate day together, we are going to try the white wine Feudi di San Gregorio 2021, which we looked at briefly above as one of the new wave of Italian white wines, but in its more exclusive (and expensive) 2012 bottling, made from organically-grown grapes. This is the later 2021 bottle, also boasting a floral fragrance of chamomile with citrus and mineral flavours, and a very affordable £12.

Feudi di San Gregorio presents its history and terroir of Irpinia, near Avellino, in the South of Italy, in a distinct and recognisable way. Founded in 1986, Feudi di San Gregorio is today a symbol of the enological renaissance of Southern Italy, hence our celebration of its other expressions in the new era of winemaking. *(Tannico, 2022)*

This wine's producer requires the most thorough safeguarding of tradition; allowing the terroir's potential to thrive. The winery has over three hundred hectares of vines, in the heart of the Sorbo Serpico area, where Feudi di San Gregorio's grapes are grown at 350 to 700 metres above sea level. *(Tannico, 2022)* The cellar was completely renovated in 2004, and now houses the ingredients that make up the recipe from which the labels of Feudi di San Gregorio flourish. These are wines that represent a relaunch of an authentic oenological area - Irpinia, and that enhance the local heritage

What food to pair it with?

This is an aged white wine that will go well with fresh cheeses, and a cracking cheeseboard always needs the perfect wine as we know. It also suits grilled fishes in many varieties - white fish; baked or blue fish.

Other wines from the same winery include:

- Feudi di San Gregorio Fiano di Avellino
- Feudi di San Gregorio Greco di Tufo
- Feudo di San Gregorio Serrocielo Falanghina

(All circa £13 / USD $15)

This winery is certainly one to look out for to expand the at-home collection or to jump at on a restaurant wine menu if lucky enough to spot one of its bottlings.

TAKE AWAY LESSON DAY 6

How to choose an organic, natural or biodynamic wine:

For many of us, it is time to extend that ethos we apply to food and fast fashion, into what is in our wine glass. Now, there is certainly no preaching here I can assure you, I fall into as many pitfalls as the next person in terms of succumbing to mass production - but we can try to but learn about those wines making huge efforts to use less pesticides, chemical additives, and animal products, and make sure we support them.

Want to be as mindful of how you choose your wine as you are your eggs? Then here is your takeaway lesson, and some recommendations, to 'drink better' for the planet, better for workers, local businesses and almost certainly, our health:

- **Look for wines labelled natural, organic, and biodynamic**

First thing's first - look for this on the label. As we covered in the above full section on this, labels can be a bit shady in the 'natural' category so I suggest looking for evidence of organic and biodynamic certifications on the bottle instead to back up claims of natural winemaking.

- **Go Vegan**

If it is the animal ethics that has most led you to this point, then also look for the vegan label on your wine bottle. It is more and more common to find them advertised in wine shops and on restaurant menus, and means that you can assume no animal products have been used in the making of the wine. *(Refinery 29, 2021)*

- **Shop independent and support small businesses**

You know that small, independent wine shop you have seen a few times on your way to work or to do an enormous Waitrose shop? Support them, they need it. These are the most likely to stock natural wines and to know a lot about them, Vintage Roots is a great example of a friendly, online organic and natural wine store which we have mentioned a few times in this book as a crediting reference.

- **Go for quality over quantity**

I am afraid this is par for the course - you get what you pay for. Natural, organic and Biodynamic wines tend to be a little bit more expensive and you need to think of it as paying for the care and attention that has gone into making it work for the planet. I tell myself 'drink a little less.. but better.' Feel free to share that.

- **Taste the native Italian grapes**

If there is one thing we have driven home throughout this book, it's preserving the rich viticultural heritage of indigenous Italian grape varieties should be celebrated in all its glory - get to know the grape names from this book and look for them not international powerhouse names on your wine label and you can bet it will be a chance to taste an outstanding wine made from native grapes.

- **Make up your own mind**

Don't worry if it's trendy; or if it looks a little cloudy in the glass (some natural wines can be or have residue left over) or; about other people's opinion on the wine - it is a huge new market of exciting brands making their way in the world and make up your mind for yourself.

(Pebble, 2022)

GLOSSARY OF TERMS

Vitis (grapevine) - a species of vining plants in the flowering plant family Vitaceae. The study and cultivation of grapevines is called viticulture.

Saignée - a winemaking technique that is primarily used in red winemaking to concentrate a ferment by removing juice.

DAY 7

INTRODUCTION TO WINE TASTING

Granted, it takes some practice and fine tuning to develop a sommelier-level understanding of a wine's characteristics, and to voice like a pro the full range of flavours and aromas in a tasting.

That said, unless you need to appear as a professional sommelier, in all his / her narrow-eyed wisdom, then I guarantee that as a newcomer wine taster, after today you will be able to follow a basic set of steps and rules when analysing a new wine – from appearance to aromas, flavours and characteristics.

I have created a handy guide on what the experts look for and how you can mimic the traits as you learn. First thing is first, prepare accordingly and don't eat pungent food and drink in the half hour before your tasting. *(Virgin Wines, 2022)* Overpowering perfumes or cleaning products can also interfere, so try to avoid these as well - get the house cleaning and the evening perfume scent on afterwards, basically - ideally in that order.

Next up, don't be intimidated by the process. In the same way that you probably won't be great the first time you go skiing (oh wait I have never got any better) it takes a while to hone the skill of tasting wine in a step-by-step manner.

Keep at it and follow these steps that fit into three categories, for a basic appreciation, and look forward to enhancing your wine drinking experience.

- Appearance

Pour the wine into a glass and hold it against a plain, white background, allowing you to fully see the colour and clarity - the worse your eyesight, the more important this detail is I hate to say. By slightly tilting the glass at an angle, you can also see how intense the colour is, from a spectrum of water-like light white wines and colourless at the edge, to a dark garnet red which will be much older with notes of toast, nuts and leather. *(Virgin Wines, 2022)* The basic rules you can rely on are as below, for red wines:

- Purple hues = a youthful wine
- Ruby-brick shades = aged

And for white wines:

- Pale yellow - green shades = youthful
- Deep lemon - gold = aged

(Wine Family, 2018)

Another aspect of the wine, but one which needs not be taken too stringent, is the "legs" of the wine left in the glass - i.e. the remnants of wine that cling to the glass and drip down the inside.

This in fact either shows alcohol content or residual sugar, leading to viscosity in the wine. They are not an independent verifier of quality itself, nor do they make you look any more knowledgeable about a good wine, so go easy on this detail if even commenting at all. *(Wine Family, 2018)*

- Nose

Now, this is the most crucial part of wine tasting so we will be going into greater detail here - mainly because the aromas, perceived only through the nose, are a vital part of the appreciation of a wine. *(Wine Family, 2018)* You should first swirl the wine in the glass to encourage the aromas to jump out, and give it a good sniff.

At this stage, you will get an idea of the style of wine straight away and even where it's from by the notes you're smelling – for instance, toasty aromas suggest the wine has been aged in oak, while fruit notes imply it is from a hot climate wine region. *(Wine Family, 2018)*

Much like 'Eat, sleep, rave, repeat' but far more civilised, the rule is 'Sniff, swirl, sniff, repeat.' And the more complexity in the wine (and therefore quality) the more you are drawn back to repeatedly smell the diverse aromas.

Now, some of us may not be ready to use overly sommelier-type language but while on this topic, the action of smelling wine can also be called 'checking the nose.' Granted, unless in the wine world you could find yourself in an unusual predicament if you volunteer this phrase, so 'smelling the aroma' or 'sniffing wine' will also do just fine here. Whatever you want to call it, the art of doing so comes in three layers: *(Binwise, 2020)*

Fig 33. Smelling wine to detect aromas

The primary aromatic level contains the most apparent flavour of the wine - namely, its fruit flavours. It will be the first smell you notice and the first flavour on your taste buds when you get to tasting it.

For a little more explanation on the fruit flavours we touched upon in our Day 4 sniffathon, the fruits you will pick up on typically fall into two different categories: red fruit and black fruit. Wines with more black fruit flavours tend to be your more full-bodied dark red, rich wines including wines like Tempranillo, and the lighter wines like Sangiovese varieties will tend to exhibit red fruits.

Of course, there are some exceptions to this rule, but this is a fairly reliable rule if you're just getting started. In white wines, you will find the two major fruit types drawn above; tree-fruits and citrus fruits. *(Wine Folly, 2020)*

The more you taste white wine, (for research purposes of course) the more you'll discover that whites in particular will vary wildly depending on its terroir. It's almost like the whole terroirs chapter was worth writing.

The secondary level demonstrates additional aromatic characteristics of the wine. You may smell herbs, woods, florals and other earthiness related to the land the vines were grown in, and it is often described as the winemaking level, e.g the smells like the above from the winemaking processes. This layer will depend on everything from the grower's technique, to how long the wine was bottled and what type of tanks or barrels it was aged in. *(Binwise, 2020)*

Finally, the third aroma level is the subtlest of smells and flavours. They often refer to the maturation process, for example the forest floor or leather, to cereals and honey. *(Wine Family, 2018)*

These are all hints of tertiary scent that linger in the air, or normally at the end of a sip - and could also include subtleties like tobacco or a note of coffee or nuts. *(Binwise, 2020)*

A final tip is don't be afraid to stick your nose deep into the glass. However, noting how close you had to get to the wine before you started to perceive aromas would tell you how pronounced the aromas are, *(Wine Family, 2018)* and it does give an indication in generic terms of a normally lower quality wine if you need to be nose diving into it.

Wines which you can't smell much of at first, however, may be a tad 'closed' and just need some time before releasing their aromas - so in some cases repeat the cycle, swirl again and see what you get…

It takes time and skill to get good at detecting specific aromas, but if you follow the above basic rules and use the Wine Aroma Wheel from Day 2, you will increasingly find the smelling and identifying process enjoyable and successful. Training your nose in general will help, so smell as many other scents around you as possible and actively note them as practice. *(Wine Family, 2018)* This will help your recall when you smell wines later and means memory mass and vocabulary you can access quickly when wine duty calls.

- Taste

Once your nose is out of the glass, it's time to take that first precious sip. Allow air to enter your mouth as well, as this accentuates the flavours. *(Virgin Wines, 2022)* Whether you swallow the wine or are doing the 'official' version of a tasting and spitting it out, you get a good idea of the flavours and feel of the wine even in that first sip, as well as how long it lingered on your tongue afterwards.

A tip is to tilt your head forward while wine tasting – the more saliva you feel rushing to the front of your mouth, the higher the acidity in the wine. *(Virgin Wines, 2022)*

Your tongue helps you perceive 5 things:

1. Sweetness
2. Bitterness
3. Sourness
4. Umami
5. Salt

(Wine Family, 2018)

Therefore we don't 'taste' a specific fruit, we in fact smell it - the taste the sweetness, whilst the smell helps us build an appreciation of which fruit it is. The taste characteristics are also appreciated at specific spots on the tongue, for example sweetness is detected at the front tip of our tongue whilst bitterness is at the back nearer our throat. *(Wine Family, 2018)*

A dry wine contains little to no sugar, but it is common for floral and/or fruity wines to be affiliated as somewhat sweet. A tip to help you tell the difference is to dip just the very tip of your tongue into the wine, and see if you can perceive sweetness at that point. If you can taste sweetness then, there is sugar content, and if you can't, then it's dry. *(Wine Family, 2018)*

However, there are more identities that can be determined only when the wine is in your mouth. These are body, tannin, acid and finish: *(Wine Family, 2018)*

- Body

This can be quite a confusing concept, but is essentially how the wine feels in the mouth, and the weight and texture, most commonly associated with a description of a red. Alcohol adds weight, and a full-bodied wine has, therefore, higher alcohol, tannin and intensity in general.

- Tannin

This is the 'gripping' sensation that can also be found in tea i.e a stickiness to the teeth and, the stronger this sensation, we would say the higher the tannin.

- Acidity

This is really important in wine, and while too much can be unappealing, too little and a wine can feel flat - so balance is the key. A simple way to test for acid is to see how much your mouth waters after you try the wine; the more your mouth waters, the more it indicates a lot of acidity. Tilting your head slightly forward as mentioned in the above section is my top tip here.

- Finish

This is the length of time you continue experiencing the wine after you have swallowed. A long finish and continued taste on the tongue is desirable. A taste that quickly disappears is described as short, and it can leave you somewhat unsatisfied.

(Wine Family, 2018)

Once you have done the above steps, we close today with a reminder that you are looking for overall balance, intensity and complexity of flavours in the wine, as well as how long it lingered on your tongue afterwards with its finish, as above.

At this stage, you are more than ready to make an informed judgement and educational contribution to a wine's quality and better understand how this correlates to the quality and price of the bottle.

So, there we are – an almost-there informed guide on how to do a wine tasting and everything you need to know for your best sommelier impression. *(Virgin Wines, 2022)*

Fig 34. Italian icons

How to buy Italian wine Guide

I am going to close the book with a 'How-To' for buying Italian wines, and by selecting 10 that cross the huge diversity of varieties- some which are new to us and some which have had a mention already within these pages.

I hope I have provided you with a narrative of the history and evolution of Italian wine, and honour that with the closing advice on how and what I would suggest you buy.

Firstly, to conquer the right bottle for you from Italy's remarkable array of options - I would encourage you to go to each Chapter of this book and take the main take-aways of primary wines associated with each area of Italy, and the indigenous grape varieties the regions are known for. If you look for your chosen wine region and the primary grape grown there, you can't go too far wrong.

Italy's wines are generally very well-priced too, and you are unlikely to come across a wine with an exorbitant price point without looking for it intentionally.

Some of the following are the "defining wines of Italy" that you will now recognise and hopefully add to your 'must-buys' when you have the opportunity, and others are protagonists of Italy's wine exports or represent the poster child of quality and craftsmanship from specific regions.

Each of them represents a tiny piece in the puzzle of the border and beautiful world of vino Italiano. Salute my friends, it has been a total pleasure.

- Tenuta San Guido Sassicaia

This wine was mentioned in the very opening pages, as in many ways, Sassicaia put Italy on the world enological map. So it is first place in my list that has completely no order anyway.

In 1968, when it broke onto the wine scene, it marked the birth of what is now commonly known as the 'super Tuscan' that put Italy on par with Bordeaux. *(Wine Enthusiast, 2022)* It is an expression of Cabernet Sauvignon with a small percent of Cabernet Franc from coastal Tuscany and my favourite story is of the Tenuta San Guido winery, managed by Nicolò Incisa della Rocchetta, representing the quality that makes it arguably Italy's number one red. *(Wine Enthusiast, 2022)*

- Ornellaia

Tenuta dell'Ornellaia is another wine that has powered the reputation of the Tuscan wine scene. OK fine there is some order to this I guess.

Ornellaia from Tenuta dell'Ornellaia in Bolgheri remains one of the top-scoring wines across several professional studies (results not needed - try for yourselves) and delivers near perfect results year after year.

Winemaker Axel Heinz mixes improvements to technology and the true tastes of this terroir. It has aromas of black cherry, spice and dark chocolate with an extraordinary richness and intensity. *(Wine Enthusiast, 2022)*

- Siddùra Spèra 2019 | Vermentino di Gallura DOCG

From the best wine white wine-producing area of Sardinia, this DOCG wine is of assuredly high quality, with flavours of lemons, pears and some minerality. It is a signature example of Vermentino, Sardinia's leading white grape, and if you are to try just one wine from the island then I recommend this be it.

The grapes for this wine are picked by hand in a vineyard in the foothills of the mountains and fermented at a low temperature in stainless steel tanks. *(The Independent, 2020)* Dino Dini, the winemaker at Siddùra, uses this technique to preserve the fresh flavours of the grape, and perfectly delivers a wine of medium body, creamy in texture and with a fruity finish. *(The Independent, 2020)*

- Mastroberardino Radici Riserva Taurasi

This wine truly shows the potential of winemaking in Southern Italy; made with Aglianico, a variety that has a long ageing life and that expresses the best of the local terroir. Symbolically, it represents the recent revival of Italy's indigenous finest grape varieties. and the revival of a grape that was close to extinction after the devastating effects of disease.

The Mastroberardino family takes credit for rediscovering and safeguarding this special resurgence *(Wine Enthusiast, 2022)*

and Taurasi is today sometimes referred to as the "Barolo of the South" *(Wine Enthusiast, 2022)* - big shoes to fill indeed. This is thanks to its sophisticated aromas and long ageing potential that has been perfectly restored. It is smoky and spicy with notes of leather, black cherry and pepper. *(Wine Enthusiast, 2022)*

- Planeta Santa Cecilia

In the far the South-East corner of Sicily is Santa Cecilia - representing the finest balance between the grape variety Nero d'Avola and its natural terroir.

As I have said a few times in this book (hopefully correctly) Sicily is the new face of Italian wines, and this one is one of my favourites.

Thanks to the hard work of vintners like Benanti and Feudo Montoni, and others we have honoured in previous chapters, the island is now getting a reputation for quality produced wines instead of just the good value labels.

This ruby-coloured red is one example and is elegant and pure with aromas of mature fruit, blackberry, herbs and pistachio to enjoy to your heart's content.. *(Wine Enthusiast, 2022)*

- Gaja Barbaresco

This wine also made it into Day 1 together.. now doesn't that feel like a lifetime ago? Cantina Gaja's achievement cannot be overlooked however - it put Barbaresco into the spotlight, and brought it international attention by building the link we now see as standard, between the grape variety Nebbiolo, its terroir and trust in a brand.

The enthusiastic vintner from Piemonte is a well-known name, and is today an international symbol for the best of Italian wine. The family business started in 1856, and Angelo came onboard in 1961 and strived for excellence in winemaking ever since.

The wine is elegant and offers notes of ripe berry fruit and soft spice - what's more you are sipping an icon of Italian wine right here. *(Wine Enthusiast, 2022)*

- Pio Cesare Barolo

We could never not have at least one Barolo in this list. Our best loved are from the area of Pio Cesare; (is that cheating really, we can't choose?) among Barolo's most historic producers with some of the most celebrated vineyards.

The Nebbiolo-based region is rich with outstanding producers such as Poderi Aldo Conterno, Fontanafredda and Michele Chiarlo. This is one of the purest expressions of an exceptional terroir, and exhibits earthy aromas of leather, spice cabinet and violets. It is a bold example of an already-bold wine, so pair it with equally bold food. *(Wine Enthusiast, 2022)*

- Feudi di Guagnano, Le Camarde Negroamaro & Primitivo 2016 Salento IGT

This is a bold and complex blend of two Southern Italian grapes - Negroamaro and Primitivo, which we delved into in more detail to reveal its synonym is Zinfadel.

This is a powerful and well developed blend, and grown on old vines ranging from 45 to 50 years of age. This is a great age-worthy wine with the potential to improve for six or seven years.

So enjoy it now, or cellar it for later if you can wait. Flavours are blackberry, prune, dark chocolate and raisins, and then sweet tobacco leading into a deliciously long finish. *(The Independent, 2020)*

- Bertani Amarone della Valpolicella Classic

Bertani Amarone Classico is a wine that has not yet reached its limits because we have yet to experience it fully by seeing its vintage The Valpolicella region, though, has certainly successfully made the switch from quantity to quality production thanks to a group of dedicated local producers.

Bertani in particular has made efforts to safeguard Amarone tradition by being among a handful of wineries in Italy to boast a full library of old and precious vintages. It has aromas of spice, mature berry fruit and smoke and the alcohol will be beautifully integrated. *(Wine Enthusiast, 2022)*

- Marchesi Antinori Tignanello

Tignanello sparked a revolution in Italy in 1971, when the first vintage of the wine was released. Then in 1900 the vineyard was purchased by Florence's Antinori family and sits within the boundaries of Chianti Classico. Rather than label it as that, Piero Antinori called the blend a "table wine." (and we all know the status offence that would cause.)

The era of the 'super Tuscan' began as a result, and Tignanello re-set the rules for a new generation of vintners. It is extraordinary on all levels and deserves recognition as the trailblazer. *(Wine Enthusiast, 2022)*

SUMMARY OF DAY 7

We have recapped on our final day together (tissues please) that Italy is a formidable force in the modern world of wine, and that you are able to conquer the world of buying and tasting it with a knowledge and understanding shaped from our time together. Today we entered into the vast subject area of wine tasting, but kept it simple to the three levels of appreciating wine; Appearance, nose and taste.

We spent slightly longer on the sense of smell and its role in wine tasting since it is the most crucial part of wine tasting and a vital part of the advanced appreciation of a wine. Plus have we even learnt anything if you don't know how to stick your nose in a glass next time you do a cellar door tour?

Next we covered how to buy Italian wine moving forwards - and a reminder that my takeaway tip would be to ensure you know your grape varieties by region (or at least your favourites ones or the most famous) and look for the native story and true identity of its terroir. There are fantastic wine magazines out there as well as wonderful independent boutiques, ready to share all of their knowledge on the world of Italian wine where you too will now find so much joy.

Next I gave you my Top 10 - in no particular order to keep you on your toes, but if looking for a quick whistle stop of a few names to throw out there as recommendations at any time, look no further than the end of this chapter for 10 wines that will impress even the hardest in life to please

DAY 7 WINE

I am going to end with something a bit different - and our final day's wine felt right to be a red - something about reds are more symbolic of an ending, shared with your dark chocolate buttons and pondering how on earth to get home now you've had one too many.

So, our final Day of the Week wine together is 'Teroldego Rotaliano Riserva, Castel Firmian 2018' - ending on a swanky high with a Riserva but at a very reasonable £16 (US$19) It is winner of a Silver Medal at the 2020 Decanter World Wine Awards, *(Eat Vita, 2022)* and I am sure many other awards before and since.

The Teroldego vine is a new one to our journey together; an indigenous variety of Trentino which we have certainly covered, but specifically from the environment in the Piana Rotaliana.

This version of the Riserva is only produced in the best vintages from specifically selected and harvested grapes in the most renowned areas of the Piana Rotaliana; namely Fron, Camorzi and Sottodossi. *(Eat Vita, 2022)*

The producer at the heart of all of it is Mezzacorona - a driving force behind the quality of the region's wines upping their game in recent years, and a winemaker executing management of a state-of-the-art winery handling estate-grown fruit from holdings in the heart of the Dolomites. *(Eat Vita, 2022)*

Add to its surely already very impressive trophy cabinet, the winery itself was also recently named 'European Winery of the Year' by Wine Enthusiast Magazine. *(Eat Vita, 2022)*

Fermentation occurred at a controlled temperature of about 25°c and then aged for a minimum of two years, of which twelve months were in oak and the rest in bottle. When you know all of these intricate details and the patience of the process, I think you will agree it is worth every penny and some - as well as our greatest of respects for the dedication.

The reason it is an interesting one to end on is that the taste is complex.. which 1) I think you can handle that now and reel off every characteristic fragrance with ease, but also 2) it is a pleasant and unusual complexity of ripe fruit aroma with prunes and blackcurrant that are a combination you don't expect but work amazingly well.

It is full-bodied and well-balanced with a soft feel in the mouth. It's time in large oak barrels, softening the tannins and concentrating the tart blackberry and vanilla flavours add to the taste appeal *(The Wine Society, 2022)*

What food to pair it with?

I haven't gone too deep into food pairings intentionally at any point throughout this book, as mainly I am no Nigella Lawson so it seems highly hypercritical, but also because it opens up a whole other subject area of wine pairing that blurs concentrating on just the wine - I will leave it to the far more critically acclaimed wine writer, but on each day have advised a general food group or dish to serve it with, in the interest of not doing totally the opposite.

And today the take away lesson will also involve an introductory basic lesson into how to pair wines generally with different types of food. For now, sticking with our wine of the day, Teroldego Rotaliano Riserva behaves in a fairly standard way of most reds in this regard, and goes well with stews as well as roasted or grilled red meats.

It is also strong enough to hold a cheese board of aged / vintage cheeses if just pairing it with a snack board. Finally, it could be ideal with rich risotto dishes and suits the richness perfectly. *(The Wine Society, 2022)*

DAY 7 TAKE AWAY LESSON

How to pair wine with different types of foods (sweet, salty, spicy, etc)

As we covered today briefly, it is our tongue that helps us perceive 5 sensations when tasting wine. To recap, those are:

1. Sweetness
2. Bitterness
3. Sourness
4. Umami
5. Salt

(Wine Family, 2018)

It is therefore these that we look for and refer to when matching wines with the right foods. At various times I may have mentioned when a wine goes particularly well with a certain meat or fish dish, like the above chosen wine today, but now we are going to look more closely at the rules which can help get you on the road to practically becoming a gastronomer and a wine pairing extraordinaire as well as a sommelier. Well almost, I'm certainly no chef I'm afraid.

Fig 34. Wine & Cheese pairing

Firstly let's understand that there are two types of wine pairing:

- Complementary pairing - which means you select a wine that will complement a dish or;
- Congruent pairing - you can drink a wine that will enhance a dish

In both cases, it is all about balance - and if that is the one takeaway from today's lesson before we even get into it - then balance (of flavours, body and alcohol) is key. *(Wine Society, 2020)* In looking at 5 general rules of wine pairing before getting to different styles of cuisine, the below are my suggested universal rules to apply when wine pairing:

1. **Keep food and wine at a similar weight and character** Lightweight food like poultry and fish are complemented by more delicate wines; medium-weight like Chardonnay go well with seafood and; rich heavier foods such as red meat need full-bodied aged red wines - all of which match the flavour and intensity of the paired wine.
2. **Know the acidity and tannin** High-acid wines can be used to cleanse the palate with oily food dishes. If you're eating a dish that already has its own strong acidic content, then pair it with a crisp dry white. Crisp, acidic wines will help to balance salty flavours, but can clash with tannin so avoid the bold red varieties.
3. **Serve a wine at least as sweet, if not sweeter than, the dish** A general sweeping rule is that you should serve a wine at least as sweet as, or sweeter than, the food being served. Sweet

foods make dry wines seem over-acidic and tart. Sweetness also balances salt which is why sweet wines are classic companions to things like cheese.

4. **Hot foods need hot wine** Spicy we mean here by hot.. Gluhwein really only has our hearts at the Christmas markets. As a rule, sweeter wines offer relief from spicy foods and we will go into further detail on this when looking at spicy cuisine matching below.
5. **Pair a dish with its sauce** Try pairing the wine to the sauce served on your dish, by using your congruent and complementary pairing techniques - yes, I think it's time for the multi-task. For example, delicate citrus sauces go well with a light white wine; cream and mushroom sauces with a middle-light rosata, and; red meat sauces with a deeper Barbaresco or similar.

(Montalto, 2022)

Now we have that under our belts, we are ready for flavour matching - Top tip here (and getting increasingly less technical) Why not take note of just the cuisines you and your family / partner / friends eat? Smart hey.

No point in me banging on about matching wines to Asian food if you last ate it in 2004, so feel free to pick those that apply to your culinary affections.

Use these simple guidelines to pair with confidence:

Flavour: Salty foods

Salty foods is a good one to start with as it is a pretty wide spectrum that lots of foods can easily fit into - particularly 'social' foods like charcuterie boards and welcome nibbles like prosciutto and anchovies etc - all of which have a salty element to them so it is likely to apply to most.

Starting with this, salt is a harmonising food component because it emphasises richness, body and fruit flavours of your wine, but also means we have two options with how to pair with it; Either… a bold tannic wine such as Barolo or Chianti which will be balanced by the salt of the food, or; A fruity acidic white wine that will add to the sensation of body and fullness to complement the saltiness of the food. *(Wine Society, 2020)*

Spicy foods

In general, remember that sweeter wines offer relief from spicy foods. If you're anything like me and need a glass of milk from even looking at a chilli, then have a sweet wine lined up soon after it. Stronger spices, such as hot chilli peppers in Thai or Indian food, i.e those that don't even apply to my palate, can clash and destroy the flavours in a wine, and typically it isn't (or probably shouldn't be) the go-to combination of an alcohol at all. But this is after all a book on wine so I will cover it.

If you choose to ignore the advice and love to ramp up the spice factor in your dishes, then you can probably also cope with a high alcohol and high tannin red. If you'd rather tone down the spice, then avoid tannic or reds and go for something with more sweetness. The milk still gets my vote.

Mildly spiced foods, such as a tagine however, will be great with a full-bodied red wine. Another life lesson from someone who needs a tonne more of them - alcohol increases the perception of alcohol burn, so bear that in mind and try to keep to a wine that is a little more modest in alcohol content. Again… milk. Just saying.

Creamy, buttery or oily food

Overly buttery or creamy foods taste delicious matched with a buttery wine - and bear with me, we might know these wines now more than you think. Think of a white grape with gutsy texture and fruit like Soave or Fiano di Avellino.

Alternatively you could try a brisk, acidic white to cut through the creaminess and cleanse your palate between mouthfuls. A young, juicy, tannic red wine variety will work well with rich, comfort foods - and we all need those some of the time. This is because tannins counteract the mouth-coating properties of the food.

Umami food

This might be a relatively new term to the Western world in some cultures, and basically means meaty, savoury foods we associate with broths and sauces of the Far East. An equivalent in other cuisines would be a slow braised beef stew and you'll know what we mean. For these we need a juicy red grape and you'll be just fine - leave the whites for fish night.

Desserts and sweets

As a basic rule for the 'afters' (do we say that anymore?) go for something with a touch of sweetness to mirror the food - a super-fruity Primitivo for example. In the same rule as before, the wine should always be sweeter than the pudding. Tropical fruits and dessert wines taste sensational with a cheese board if we are going there too FYI.

Ending on wine pairing (even IF in its simplest form of different types of food) is as high as I go in terms of life etiquette.. I don't go beyond here myself I'm afraid, and I leave you at this point, with everything I know. The best thing to remember is that food and wine pairing is subjective, and that you are most likely even more qualified than the next person, to just have a go.

Try next time you are in a restaurant or playing host, to match full-bodied wines with relatively high alcohol, with full-flavoured dishes; and stick to lighter, less alcoholic styles, with subtle flavours. *(The Wine Society, 2020)* I can tell you right now that if you keep it Italian, once people have one glass, they will have a great evening either way. Yes, there are some simple guidelines to matching food and wine.. but you know them now and they are not hard and fast. Match what you love and you will nail this.

DAY 7 GLOSSARY OF TERMS

Umami - a salty, meaty taste, traditionally associated with the intensely flavoured broths and sauces of the Far East (and literally translates as 'pleasant savoury taste' in Japanese)

CONCLUSION

As we have seen from the wealth of examples we have celebrated together in this book, Italy boasts an incredibly impressive list of enological achievements going back to early civilization's fermentations. It isn't too soon to announce that in the current climate, Italy often closes the year as the world's number one wine producer. *(Wine Enthusiast, 2022)*

Italy currently accounts for roughly one-fifth of the world's wine, and through this journey from discovering its rather complicated classification system, to the emerging trends making waves this decade and everything in between, I hope you have come away with a sense of the distinctive characteristics of the Italian regions - from Piemonte to Sicily.

Most importantly, I hope you put down this book thinking it is something you will pick up again when choosing a crisp white wine for a summer lunch, or when you need the perfect aged red as a present for that relative you find it hard to buy for.

The references to the wines we have covered will stand the test of time and be names you see well into the future. Italy delivers, and always has, many of the bottles we love and remember most, that we go to in the wine shop and will enjoy with family and friends. Hopefully now you have a broader range of these to choose from and aren't as daunted when the job of choosing one sits with you.

Rather topically, this year marks the 30th anniversary of the DOCG upper classification that cements Italy's well-earned reputation as a producer of quality wine. *(Wine Enthusiast, 2022)*

This status bestowed upon an ever- increasing number of Italian wines means it is a country creating bottles that compete with the best of Bordeaux, California and the rest of the wine-making world; those that tower over Italy in terms of production capacity and size.

This year inspires me even more, and hopefully all of you from now onwards, to reflect on how far Italy has come in three decades from a volume producer of average everyday wines, to one offering the most iconic cellar selection in the world. It has never been a more exciting time to invest your attention, care and money - on the gloriously sophisticated and varied realm of Italian winemaking in all its wholesome glory. For the hundredth and now final time I promise.. Salute!

Go out there and taste, smell, choose, pair wines with confidence - but more importantly, drink boldly!

LEAVE A REVIEW!

Customer reviews

1

5.0 out of 5 stars

5 star		100%
4 star		0%
3 star		0%
2 star		0%
1 star		0%

See all 1 customer reviews

Share your thoughts with other customers

Write a customer review

LIST OF IMAGES

REFERENCES

Introduction and Day 1

G. (2021, March 30). The consortium. Consorzio Vino Chianti. https://www.consorziovinochianti.it/the-consortium/?lang=en

F. (2017, August 7). History of Italian Wine Industry. Via Verdi. https://viaverdimiami.com/history-of-italian-wine-industry/

Farrow, S. (2020). 7 Italian winemakers you need to know. The Wine Society. https://www.thewinesociety.com/discover/explore/grower-stories/7-italian-winemakers-you-need-to-know

F.D. (2022). How to read the label of wines with designation of origin. Federdoc. https://www.federdoc.com/en/how-to-read-the-label-of-wines-with-designation-of-origin/

The Italian Wine | History, Regions, Classification. (2022). Vino e Camino. https://www.vinoecamino.it/italian-wine/

Larner, M. (2010, March 31). 15 Icons of Italian Wine. Wine Enthusiast. https://www.winemag.com/2010/03/31/15-icons-of-italian-wine/

M. (2020, November 8). Italian Wine Guide: Explore the 20 Wine Regions of Italy - 2022. MasterClass. https://www.masterclass.com/articles/italian-wine-guide#a-brief-history-of-italian-winemaking

Peartree, A. (2021, August 3). The Italian Winemakers Reviving an Ancient Region. Wine Enthusiast. https://www.winemag.com/2021/08/03/italian-wine-region-vulture-guide/

A quick history of Italian wine. (2019). Cult Wines. https://www.wineinvestment.com/learn/magazine/2019/07/a-quick-history-of-italian-wine/

Robinson, J. (2016). The 24-Hour Wine Expert (Illustrated ed.). Abrams Image.

SevenFifty Daily Editors & SevenFifty Daily Editors. (2018, November 19). Italian Wine Today: What You Need to Know. SevenFifty Daily. https://daily.sevenfifty.com/italian-wine-today-what-you-need-to-know/#:%7E:

text=Wine%20has%20been%20made%20in,trade%20throughout%20the%20their%20empire%2C

Vineyards Media. (2022). Italy map of vineyards wine regions. https://vineyards.com/wine-map/italy

Day 2

C. (2021a, December 14). *Piqueras Wineries*. Bodegas Piqueras. https://www.bodegaspiqueras.com/en/

editorial staff. (2019, April 16). *THE PYRAMID OF QUALITY. DOCG & DOC*. My Name Is Barbera. https://www.mynameisbarbera.com/the-pyramid-of-quality-the-docg/

F.D. (2022). *The pyramid of italian wines*. Federdoc. https://www.federdoc.com/en/the-pyramid-of-italian-wines/

Italianowine. (2018, August 9). *DOCG appellation*. https://www.italianowine.com/en/classification/appellations/docg/

M. (2021b). *What Is DOC and DOCG Wine? Differences Between DOC, DOCG, IGT, and VdT on Italian Wine Labels*. Masterclass. https://www.masterclass.com/articles/what-is-doc-and-docg-wine-differences-between-doc-docg-igt-and-vdt-on-italian-wine-labels

Miller-Wilson, K., More, R., & More, R. (2022, May 5). *How to Use a Wine Tasting Wheel*. LoveToKnow. https://wine.lovetoknow.com/wine-tasting-wheel

Silverstein, Michael. (2019). 8. Semiotic Vinification and the Scaling of Taste. 10.1525/9780520965430-011.

Tips on Tasting: Wine Bouquet vs Aroma. (2022). Wine Folly. https://winefolly.com/tips/tips-on-tasting-wine-bouquet-vs-aroma/

Wine Aroma Wheel - Part 2. (2009, March 15). [Video]. YouTube. https://www.youtube.com/watch?v=2skRwwR5Nbk

Wine Aroma Wheel: Describe Your Wine Without Feeling Snobby. (2020, October 23). Usual. https://usualwines.com/blogs/knowledge-base/wine-aroma-wheel

Day 3

Vineyards Media. (2022). Italy map of vineyards wine regions. https://vineyards.com/wine-map/italy

E. (2022a). *Wine Styles*. Wine-Searcher. https://www.wine-searcher.com/styles

F.D. (2022b). *How to read the label of wines with designation of origin*. Federdoc. https://www.federdoc.com/en/how-to-read-the-label-of-wines-with-designation-of-origin/

Robillard, H. (2022). *Vinovest | Investing in Wine as an Alternative Asset*. Vinovest. https://www.vinovest.co/blog/italian-wine-regions

Sorrentino, L. (2022, March 28). *Italy Wine Regions and Wines: A Beginners Guide for Foodies*. Italy Foodies. https://www.italyfoodies.com/blog/italy-wine-regions

Vigh, K. (2022). *Italian Wine Regions â Discover the Wines of Italy | Total Wine & More*. Total Wine & More. https://www.totalwine.com/content/learn/italian-wine-regions

Day 4

Asimov, E. (2014, March 27). Traipsing the Terroir of Nebbiolo. The New York Times. https://www.nytimes.com/2014/04/02/dining/traipsing-the-terroir-of-nebbiolo.html

E. (2022a, August 14). The clones of sangiovese in Tuscany. Vino Travels Italy. http://www.vinotravelsitaly.com/2015/02/the-clones-of-sangiovese-in-tuscany.html

Editor. (2018, May 25). Especially Puglia. Especially Puglia. https://www.especiallypuglia.com/general/wines-of-puglia-guide/

Howard, P. (2020a, October 2). Vermentino di Sardegna DOC, Part 2. Wine Alchemy. https://www.winealchemy.co.uk/vermentino-di-sardegna-doc-part-2/

Howard, P. (2020b, October 3). Vermentino di Sardegna DOC, Part 1. Wine Alchemy. https://www.winealchemy.co.uk/vermentino-di-sardegna-doc-pt-1/

Howard, P. (2020c, October 30). Italy's Native Wine Grape Terroirs – Book Review. Wine Alchemy. https://www.winealchemy.co.uk/

italys-native-wine-grape-terroirs-by-ian-dagata-book-review/

Identifying Flavors in Wine. (2022). Wine Folly. https://winefolly.com/deep-dive/identifying-flavors-in-wine/

Johnson, B. (2022). Smelling Wine: 5 Steps of How To Smell Wine Professionally. Bin Wise. https://home.binwise.com/blog/smelling-wine

Red wine » Terre dei Vestini DOC » Italian Wine Guide. (2022). Italian Wine Guide. https://italianwine.guide/regions-en-gb/abruzzo-en-gb/montepulciano-dabruzzo-terre-dei-vestini-doc/

SevenFifty Daily Editors & SevenFifty Daily Editors. (2021, May 14). How Northern Italy is Carving a New Niche for Terroir-Driven White Wine. SevenFifty Daily. https://daily.sevenfifty.com/how-northern-italy-is-carving-a-new-niche-for-terroir-driven-white-wine/

Shannon, E., Shannon, E., Shannon, E., & Shannon, E. (2014). What is "Terroir"? – Uncorked In Italy Italian Natural Wine. Uncorked in Italy. https://uncorkedinitaly.com/what-is-terroir/

Stuteley, G. (2018, July 3). What's best for Italian wine its unique grape varieties or its regions asks Gordon Stuteley of GS Wines. The Buyer. http://www.the-buyer.net/people/gordon-stuteley-of-gs-wines-looks-at-italys-unique-grape-varietals-and-wine-terroirs/

V. (2022b, August 14). The terroir of Italy and the wines it produces. Vino Travels in Italy. http://www.vinotravelsitaly.com/2015/02/the-terrior-of-italy.html

Zhang, A. (2022). Vinovest | Investing in Wine as an Alternative Asset. Vinovest. https://www.vinovest.co/blog/primitivo

ZHANG, A. N. T. H. O. N. Y. (2022). Vinovest | Investing in Wine as an Alternative Asset. Vinovest. https://www.vinovest.co/blog/montepulciano-dabruzzo#l*ink-2*

Day 5

(2022, March 16). Lugana, 100% Turbiana - Pratello (75cl) Lombardy.

ViTA. https://eatvita.co.uk/shop/beers-wines-and-spirits/lugana-100-turbiana-pratello-75cl-lombardy/

Masterclass. (2021). Italian Wine Grape Guide: 21 Wine Grapes That Grow in Italy. https://www.masterclass.com/articles/italian-wine-grape-guide

Robillard, H. (2022). Vinovest | Investing in Wine as an Alternative Asset. Vinovest. https://www.vinovest.co/blog/italian-wine-regions#link-14

Roots, V. (2022a, July 22). Top 6 Italian Wine Regions and Grapes. Vintage Roots: Organic Wine | Biodynamic Wines. https://www.vintageroots.co.uk/wine-guides/italian-wine-regions-and-grapes-map-included/

S. (2020, August 22). Wine Region Overview: Northern Italy. Briscoe Bites. http://briscoebites.com/wine-region-overview-northern-italy/

Day 6

13 Common Light Red Wine Varieties. (2022). Wine Folly. https://winefolly.com/deep-dive/light-red-wine/

Asimov, E. (2016, July 20). From Etna and the Salty Sea, a White of Great Potential. The New York Times. https://www.nytimes.com/2016/07/20/dining/mount-etna-wine-sicily.html

Broggi, M. (2021, May 21). 5 Trending Italian White Grape Varieties. Wine Scholar Guild. https://www.winescholarguild.org/blog/5-trending-italian-white-grape-varieties

Button, J. (2022, April 13). The new Super-Italians: 12 essential, new-wave Italian wines. Decanter. https://www.decanter.com/premium/the-new-super-italians-12-essential-new-wave-italian-wines-477929/

By The Newsroom. (2018, June 8). RICHARD ESLING: Could this be the new wave Italian wine for the UK? SussexWorld. https://www.sussexexpress.co.uk/news/opinion/columnists/richard-esling-could-this-be-the-new-wave-italian-wine-for-the-uk-1099434

Clark, C. (2019, September 13). Meet the Young Winemakers Championing Barolo's New Wave. VinePair. https://vinepair.com/articles/new-wave-barolo-winemakers/

Csanady, A. (2021, February 16). How To Apply Your Ethical Fashion Values To Buying Wine. Refinery29. https://www.refinery29.com/en-gb/2021/02/10313070/best-wine-organic-biodynamic-uk

Donadoni, L. (2021, November 3). Ageing Italian white wines? Yes you can, here the grape varietis to look for. . . The Italian Wine Girl. https://theitalianwinegirl.com/ageing-italian-white-wines-yes-you-can-here-the-grape-varietis-to-look-for/

D'Vari, M. (2019, July 15). Chiaretto: The Italian Rosé Wine. Forbes. https://www.forbes.com/sites/marisadvari/2019/07/15/chiaretto-the-italian-ros-wine/?sh=3732f9e84f64

E. (2021). Sustainably maintaining Italy's wine tradition, despite a changing climate. Sygenta Group. https://www.syngentagroup.com/en/our-stories/sustainably-maintaining-italys-wine-tradi tion-despite-changing-climate

E. (2022a). Nebbiolo di Carema Carema | Vivino. Vivino. https://www.vivino.com/GB/en/carema-carema/w/1267706

E. (2022b). Wine By Country - Italy - Italian Orange Wine - Wayward Wines. Wayward Wines. https://waywardwines.co.uk/italian-orange-natural-wine/

Everything You Want to Know About Orange Wine. (2022). Wine Folly. https://winefolly.com/deep-dive/orange-wine/

Feudi di San Gregorio. (2022). Tannico. https://www.tannico.co.uk/winery/feudi-di-san-gregorio.html

Finetti, M. (2022, March 22). What is Carema? Ask. Decanter. https://www.decanter.com/learn/what-is-carema-ask-decanter-475667/

Jarvis, T. (2018, September 23). Hybrids, Crossings and Foxy Wines | Technical Articles. Wine-Searcher. https://www.wine-searcher.com/m/2018/09/hybrids-crossings-and-foxy-wines

Jenssen, M. D. A. J. (2018, October 16). The Truth Behind Your Favorite Wines. Wine Enthusiast. https://www.winemag.com/2018/10/16/truth-behind-wine-grape-crosses-hybrids/

Larner, M. (2010, March 31). 15 Icons of Italian Wine. Wine Enthusiast. https://www.winemag.com/2010/03/31/15-icons-of-italian-wine/

Magazine, P. (2018, March 5). 8 expert tips for choosing natural wine. Pebble Magazine. https://pebblemag.com/magazine/eating-drinking/expert-tips-for-choosing-natural-wine-raw-wine-fair

Mazzeo, J. (2021, December 14). EU grants member states the right to use resistant hybrid varieties in appellation wines. Decanter. https://www.decanter.com/wine-news/eu-grants-member-states-the-right-to-use-resistant-hybrid-varieties-in-appellation-wines-470864/

Micallef, J. V. (2018, May 28). Exploring The World Of Italian Rosé. Forbes. https://www.forbes.com/sites/joemicallef/2018/05/27/exploring-the-world-of-italian-rose/?sh=592302533406

Mullen, T. (2017, July 10). The Mother-Daughter Team Rocking Italy's Wine Scene. Forbes. https://www.forbes.com/sites/tmullen/2017/07/10/the-mother-daughter-team-rocking-italys-wine-scene/

New Wave White Wines of Southern Italy. (2019, November 4). Wine Enthusiast. https://www.winemag.com/gallery/southern-italys-new-wave-whites/

Olsen, B. (2022, May 24). 10 best orange wines to raise a glass to this summer. The Independent. https://www.independent.co.uk/extras/indybest/food-drink/wine/best-orange-wine-buy-italy-spain-organic-brands-bottles-uk-a9651071.html

Organic, Biodynamic, Natural Wines in Italy | Italian Organic Wineries. (2022, April 19). VinoBio. https://www.vino-bio.com/en/

Parr, D. (2021, October 11). How a New Generation of Wine Pros Are Positioning Sicily to be the Next Great Italian Wine Region. VinePair. https://vinepair.com/articles/next-generation-sicilian-wine-pros/

Robinson, J. (2022). Nebbiolo. Jancis Robinson. https://www.jancisrobinson.com/learn/grape-varieties/red/nebbiolo

Roviello, V., Caruso, U., dal Poggetto, G., & Naviglio, D. (2021). Hybrid Grapes for a Sustainable Viticulture in South Italy: Parentage Diagram Analysis and Metal Assessment in a Homemade Wine of Chambourcin Cultivar. Sustainability, 13(22), 12472. https://doi.

org/10.3390/su132212472

Staff, W. (2022, April 11). Aglianico - Piedirosso Wine. Wine-Searcher. https://www.wine-searcher.com/grape-1974-aglianico-piedirosso

TasteAtlas. (2021, January 13). Asolo Prosecco | Local Wine Appellation From Province of Treviso, Italy | TasteAtlas. https://www.tasteatlas.com/asolo-prosecco

V. (2022c, January 4). Italy's best natural wines. Gourmet Hunters Blog. https://www.gourmethunters.com/blog/en/italys-best-natural-wines/

What is Orange Wine? (2020, January 13). Eataly. https://www.eataly.com/us_en/magazine/how-to/what-is-orange-wine/

Wilson, C. (2021, July 20). Light-bodied Italian red wines: 10 top bottles worth seeking out. Decanter. https://www.decanter.com/premium/light-bodied-italian-red-wines-10-top-bottles-worth-seeking-out-459032/

Day 7

A. (2022a, July 7). Teroldego Rotaliano Riserva, Castel Firmian - Mezzacorona (75cl) Trentino Region. ViTA. https://eatvita.co.uk/shop/new-arrival/teroldego-rotaliano-riserva-castel-firmian-mezzacorona-75cl-trentino-region/

A. (2022b, July 7). Teroldego Rotaliano Riserva, Castel Firmian - Mezzacorona (75cl) Trentino Region. ViTA. https://eatvita.co.uk/shop/new-arrival/teroldego-rotaliano-riserva-castel-firmian-mezzacorona-75cl-trentino-region/

Allen, R. (2020, June 15). An easy guide to matching food and wine. The Wine Society. https://www.thewinesociety.com/discover/wine-basics/serve-store-taste/an-easy-guide-to-matching-food-and-wine

Eaton, Z. (2022, March 31). 8 simple rules for matching food and wine. Montalto. https://montalto.com.au/8-rules-for-matching-food-and-wine/

Family, W. (2018, May 11). Wine Tasting 101 - The Basics Of What To

Do & Say. Wine-Family.Com. https://wine-family.com/blogs/news/wine-tasting-101-the-basics-of-what-to-do-say

Geek, W. (2022, June 28). The complete guide to the best Italian wine with maps and tasting notes. Independent Wine. https://www.independent.wine/2020/04/07/the-ultimate-guide-to-the-best-italian-wine/

How to Taste Wine | Wine Guide. (2022, April 26). Virgin Wines. https://www.virginwines.co.uk/hub/wine-guide/wine-basics/how-to-taste-wine/

Italian Red Wines. (2022). The Wine Society. https://www.thewinesociety.com/buy/wines/red-wine/italy

Johnson, B. (2022). Smelling Wine: 5 Steps of How To Smell Wine Professionally. Bin Wise. https://home.binwise.com/blog/smelling-wine

Knowles, S. (2021, January 3). The ultimate guide to Italian wine. The Wine Society. https://www.thewinesociety.com/discover/explore/regional-guides/italian-wine-ultimate-guide

Larner, M. (2010a, March 31). 15 Icons of Italian Wine. Wine Enthusiast. https://www.winemag.com/2010/03/31/15-icons-of-italian-wine/

Larner, M. (2010b, March 31). 15 Icons of Italian Wine. Wine Enthusiast. https://www.winemag.com/2010/03/31/15-icons-of-italian-wine/

www.ingramcontent.com/pod-product-compliance
Ingram Content Group UK Ltd.
Pitfield, Milton Keynes, MK11 3LW, UK
UKHW020631300125
4364UKWH00040B/674